The Great Aussie
Pub Crawl

The Great Aussie
Pub Crawl

Douglass Baglin • Yvonne Austin

CHILD & ASSOCIATES
AN ALL-AUSTRALIAN PUBLISHER

Acknowledgements

We wish to express our hearty thanks and appreciation to all the people who helped us on our pub crawl, the 'characters' who made some pubs better than others and the fine 'mine hosts' and barmaids who make many people's lives more pleasant. We pay a special tribute to the memory of those men and women who constructed such beautiful buildings and gave to them a personality unique to this country.

Our many thanks to our forebears who taught us the art of happy pub crawling, and to the numerous people who encouraged us to experience various hotels all over Australia.

To all the publicans who went to so much trouble to supply us with information about their hotels and things of interest, we offer thanks and congratulations.

Most of all, our thanks to all the people who drink in pubs, for it is by their patronage that the Australian pub has survived.

The poem, 'A Pub Without Beer', is reproduced on page 8 by kind permission of Mrs Shaun Sheahan.

Front endpaper: *Obtaining supplies, eastern goldfields, Western Australia.*

Back endpaper: *Flags fly from the Tattersalls Hotel, Hay, New South Wales.*

Front cover: *Perched on the open plains beside Highway 31, just north of Albury, New South Wales, is the Ettamogah Pub. Cartoonist Ken Maynard, who was born at Albury, established the pub in his comic strip in* Australasian Post *over twenty years ago. The fun and humour it generated inspired Lindsay 'Coop' Cooper and his wife Sonia to build the pub. With its old Chevrolet utility (deposited in a flood), the dog Bandit outside his kennel, barmen dressed in their best stubbies, boots and black singlets, the pub opened in 1987 and is constantly flocked by tourists.*

Half-title: *The Long Yard Hotel outside Tamworth, New South Wales, was designed by the architectural firm Jackson Teece Chesterman Willis and Partners and built in 1985. It is the first stage of a huge complex which will include a 4000-seat auditorium, restaurant, motel, markets, stores, recording studios and sporting facilities.*

Half-title verso: *Inns of old usually displayed well-illustrated signs depicting the name of the public house for those who couldn't read. The Coach and Horses Inn, a large two-storey bluestone building with two rear wings and large stable block, was built between 1856 and 1857 and was one of Cobb & Co.'s resting places between Melbourne and the goldfields.*

Title: *The famous Breakfast Creek Hotel, Brisbane, was built in 1889, on the spot where John Oxley is supposed to have landed and had breakfast during the voyage on which he discovered the Brisbane River. A conglomeration of styles, the hotel is one of Brisbane's landmarks.*

Published by Child & Associates Publishing Pty Ltd,
5 Skyline Place, Frenchs Forest, NSW, Australia, 2086
Telephone (02) 975 1700, facsimile (02) 975 1711
A wholly owned Australian publishing company
This book has been edited, designed and typeset in Australia by the publisher
First edition 1990
© Douglass Baglin and Yvonne Austin 1990
Edited by James Young
Printed in Singapore by Toppan Printing Co. (S) Pte Ltd
Typesetting processed by Deblaere Typesetting Pty Ltd

**National Library of Australia
Cataloguing-in-Publication Data**

Baglin, Douglass.
The great Aussie pub crawl.

ISBN 0 86777 037 6.

1. Pub architecture—Australia. 2. Hotels, taverns, etc.—Australia. I. Austin, Yvonne. II. Title.

728.50994

Like so many outback Queensland pubs, the Railway and Artesian Hotels at Barcaldine, near Longreach, have a rambling spaciousness, verandahs being their main feature. It was under the gum in front of the Railway Hotel that shearers involved in the famous 1891 strike held a meeting, from which the Australian Labour Party was formed. It endorsed Thomas Ryan, a fellow striker who became the world's first Labour parliamentarian. The armed strikers' camp, under the flag of Eureka, was 2 kilometres from the railway station and is immortalised in Henry Lawson's 'Freedom of the Wallaby'

> We'll make the tyrants feel the sting
>   Of those that they would throttle;
> They needn't say the fault is ours
>   If blood should stain the wattle.

Standing by itself on a lonely stretch of track is the Royal Hotel at Tambar Springs, 70 kilometres east of Coonabarabran, New South Wales. Pubs such as these are important meeting places in those areas where social activities are limited.

Introduction

An Australian pub crawl is a pleasant trip through a fascinating country where one is continually surprised and awed by the vastness of our nation and by the contrast of the landscape and the wildly differing climate; where forms and patterns are ever changing in a kaleidoscope of colour and light.

Australia's history has been dramatically shaped by pubs. After the arrival of the First Fleet, illegal grog houses sprang up like mushrooms. To control the chaos that these wrought and to regulate the behaviour of those early guests, laws were hastily established and reshaped. However, grog was the colony's currency.

When those who ventured in search of good land reported favourably of their finds, people radiated from the colony centres and began farming or grazing. Inns to facilitate some of these settlers and travellers were established on roadsides at intervals of a day's horse ride. As communities formed, pubs were built and grew in size and number as the town expanded. Their locations were mostly determined by the population movement and type of transport and their style was largely a product of climate and the building materials available. In southern areas where winters were bleak, small cosy rooms with fireplaces were common while the northern pubs, surrounded by wide shady verandahs, sprawled out, forming fascinating streetscapes.

Today, throughout Australia, the landscape is dotted with pubs. But the pub is not just a building, it is a social experience—alive with the noise of slurping and guzzling, of glasses hitting the counter top, of talk, laughter and arguments. A place where men and women can relax, do business, look for work, have a meal or just a quiet drink. The pub provides company and news for people who live in isolated areas, some lonely, many shy. Like its customers, the outback pub is generally welcoming, basic and practical with a charm not found elsewhere. Whether it be a substantial building with large verandahs set amongst the trees or a humble pub on some lonely dusty road, its furniture is generally simple, its publican generous, but firm, its operation friendly and its beer cold.

In country towns usually the largest and often the most beautiful buildings are the pubs. In many towns the pub is the town. Varying in style, material and decor, each has its own personality. Some are strong, warm honey-coloured sandstone buildings, delicately laced with beautiful iron verandahs; others are of timber or brick with iron roofs and distinctive wooden balconies. The pub is a favourite place for travelling salesmen who can have a good counter lunch, a beer and a chat. It provides a meeting place for rural workers and townspeople. What the townsfolk demand as a service sets the standard.

Tragically, many beautiful old pubs have been demolished or torn apart and robbed of their charm. Their downfall is often caused by pressure from townsfolk who wish to portray a 'modern' image. A sameness is encroaching on something that was once unique. This sameness has the distinction only of being ugly or completely out of character with the surrounds.

City pubs are governed largely in style and service by the price of city real estate and the demands of hurried business people. Usually in prominent places, these skyscrapers with their plush decor and stereotyped accommodation, bars, restaurants, swimming pools and saunas, provide fine service for big prices. Sometimes small gems, tucked away among the towering glass and concrete office blocks, provide a welcome escape.

In contrast, beach hotels emphasise boobs and bottoms, which bounce their way around bars and beer gardens to the sound of taped music. Like the resort hotels, their trade is generally dependent on weather and season.

Laws, placing restrictions on hotels and public, vary from State to State. They have affected the architecture, the facilities and the drinking habits of the consumer. Ultimately it is the consumer whose demands cause changes and set standards.

Our bias in this book is obvious. We have tried to present as wide a range of Australian pubs as possible. For the most part they are the great old pubs, the small country hostelries, the tiny outback 'sheds', that have made this country the great place for pubs that it is. The services they offer will certainly continue to flourish; we hope that the pubs themselves will continue to flourish too.

In his book, *Songs from the Canefields*, Dan Sheahan describes the black day at Ingham after the battle of the Coral Sea when the old Day Dawn Hotel was 'a pub without beer'—its entire supply had been sold to the Americans:

Old swing doors, once common in most Queensland pubs, are rarely seen today. This doorway of the Union Hotel at Miles, 350 kilometres north-west of Brisbane, advertises old labels.

Opposite page: The window of the Queen's Head Hotel at Wilcannia, New South Wales. The old hotel, built in the 1870s, has recently closed. In its heyday the town had many pubs, grog shanties and breweries, all of which served the thousands of diggers who arrived by riverboat and on the 30–40 weekly coaches heading through to the nearby Mt Browne goldfields.

The lovely brick and stone Hotel Central at Riverton has a distinctive verandah and balcony and quaint accompanying residence. Riverton is a small agriculture town 100 kilometres north of Adelaide which came into being in 1855 when grazier James Masters subdivided a portion of his land on the Gilbert River.

It is lonely away from your kindred and all
In the bushland at night when the warrigals call—
It is sad by the sea where the wild breakers boom
Or to look on a grave and contemplate doom.
But there's nothing on earth half as lonely and drear
As to stand in the bar of a pub without beer.

Madam with her needles sits still by the door—
The boss smokes in silence—he is joking no more
There's a faraway look on the face of the bum
While the barmaid glares down at the paint on her
    thumb.
The cook has gone cranky and the yardman is queer
Oh, a terrible place is a pub without beer.

Once it stood by the wayside all stately and proud—
'Twas a home to the loafers—a joy to the crowd—
Now all silent the roof-tree that oftentimes rang
When the navvies were paid and the cane-cutters sang.
Some are sleeping their last in the land far from here
and I feel all alone in a pub without beer.

They can hang to their coupons for sugar and tea
And the shortage of sandshoes does not worry me—
And though benzine and razors be both frozen stiff
What is wrong with the horse and the old-fashioned
    ziff.
'Mid the worries of war there's but one thing I fear
'Tis to stand in the bar of a pub without beer.

Oh, you brew of brown barley, what charm is thine?
'Neath thy spell men grow happy and cease to repine.
The cowards become brave and the weak become strong
The dour and the grumpy burst forth into song.
If there's aught to resemble high heaven down here
'Tis the palace of joy where they ladle out beer.

*Menus decorate the facade of the Yacht Club Hotel at Williamstown,
Melbourne. The cook, Mrs Emma Hallcroft, has created wonderful
meals at cheap prices for thirty years during the reign of eleven
publicans. The most meals served in one day was 972 and the record
for a week 4495.*

*In December 1877, Frederick Musika requested the removal of
the licence from the Old Post Office Inn to a house to be known as
the Lord Clyde Hotel. Carlton and West End Brewery built this
hotel in place of the old Lord Clyde and Mr T. Durham became its
publican. A big sign 'Sorry. No Pub Crawls Served in this Hotel'
tells its own story.*

The Commercial Hotel at Biloela in the Callide Valley, 150 kilometres south of Rockhampton, Queensland, is in the midst of dairy and beef-producing country with some coalmining.

Left: *At a railway siding near Nyngan, a small town on the Bogan River north-west of Dubbo, New South Wales, stands the Gateway Hotel. On these flat plains, wool, lambs and wheat are grown, and on hot summer days this pub becomes a popular place.*

Top: *A storm lurks over the lovely town of Glen Innes, New South Wales, on the New England Tablelands. Scottish folk were first to settle in the area which became known as 'Beardy Plains'. In 1852 the town was gazetted and named after Major A. C. Innes, former commandant of the penal settlement at Port Macquarie. Nearby tin mines attracted miners to the district, which gained attention when the bushranger Captain Thunderbolt was tried in the court.*

The Club Hotel, a two-storey building with lace balcony, was erected in 1906.

XXXX on tap.

Sydney's Gresham Hotel harmonises with its surrounding buildings: the Town Hall, St Andrew's Cathedral and the Queen Victoria Building. Sandstone door and window surrounds and gables decorate the five-storey red brick Victorian building, which was designed by J. Kirkpatrick and built in 1890 as a bank and offices.

The attractive Wellington Hotel at Wellington, New South Wales, was built in 1900 and is the waterhole for the nearby rural community.

Situated at the confluence of the Bell and Macquarie Rivers, the valley was named by explorer John Oxley in 1817 after the Duke of Wellington. In 1823 a convict workforce was established and settlers began taking up land along the rivers. The town was laid out in 1846.

Top: *This attractive pub is in harmony with its idyllic surroundings, among beautiful straight eucalypts in one of Tasmania's most spectacular wilderness areas. Nearby is Tasmania's Cradle Mountain–Lake St Clair National Park, comprising over 126 000 hectares of magnificent country, incorporating Australia's deepest freshwater, glacier-formed lake, which is also the source of the Derwent River.*

On the hot red Queensland plains 180 kilometres north of Warri Warri gate near Camerons Corner is the welcoming sight of the Noccundra Hotel. In 1920 it was built of stone quarried at Mt Poole Station and replaced a hotel which stood from the 1870s to service workers at Nockatunga Station.

The former township of Noccundra has dissipated, the population having dropped from 400 to 4, so as well as providing refreshments for stationhands and oil workers from the nearby Jackson and Watson oilfields, the hotel sells petrol, diesel, spare vehicle parts and food provisions. The Royal Flying Doctor Service, with doctors and dentists from Broken Hill, visits the hotel once a month to attend to the needs of people on outlying properties. The hotel is one of the oldest standing buildings in the south-west Queensland.

Good fun and good humour! Combo Hotel, Winton, Queensland.

In the red dusty arid west amid the Barrier Range, the Silverton Hotel, built of stone in 1885 near Broken Hill, New South Wales, makes a welcome relief on a hot day. A canvas shanty town that boomed in the late 1880s, Silverton became almost deserted when the mineral wealth of Broken Hill became known.

Below: *Melbourne's wonderful Windsor! In 1847 the White Hart Inn stood where the State Houses of Parliament now stand. On land beside it, Charles Webb's design for the Grand Hotel began to take shape in 1883. Grand in every aspect, it prospered until 1886 when purchased by James Munro (a later Premier) who, at a banquet, burnt its licence before a roomful of teetotal guests. Renamed the Temperance Coffee Palace, it was extended for the 1888 Great Exhibition. In 1920 a group led by Sir John Monash arranged a paper merger between the licensed, but demolished, White Hart and the Grand. A licence was issued for the Grand, renamed the Windsor.*

Below left: *The impressive crest over the doorway of Melbourne's famous Windsor Hotel.*

The Grog Begins to Flow

A crawl back through the history of our pubs is almost as interesting and fascinating as a day-by-day crawl from pub to pub. It seems we have inherited at least one trait of our ancestors—the love of liquor. It began just over two centuries ago when the shores of Australia were blessed with a shipment of grog-lovers. A day after their arrival in Sydney Cove, glasses were raised, the flag saluted, a toast proposed and cheers resounded as the first alcohol on Australian soil was officially drunk.

Aboard the anchored ships of the First Fleet were packed the government's guests, that carefully selected mass of unpatriotic, unskilled unwanteds—Australia's stud stock—the backbone of our nation! Stored also, with much more love and care, was the valuable three-year supply of spirits and wines which Secretary Nepean had instructed was to be rationed to the marines, military and civil officers. The well-woven web of convicts, military men and liquor which resulted was aggravated by lust and greed and became a key factor in shaping the course of Australia's history, architecture, laws and lifestyle.

As convicts were landed, daily routines and tasks were set. As part of the marines' remuneration, a daily ration of rum was allotted. To those transported and about to embark on their sentence, alcoholic pleasures were forbidden. It wasn't long before some of these artisans of crime stole what they regarded as a natural part of everyday life—grog! Those whose thirsts remained unquenched began bartering their precious food rations and selling their services and assets cheaply for meagre amounts of alcohol obtained from corrupt and opportunist officers. The number of men far outstretched the number of women, and prostitution, mostly for the payment of rum, was rife.

The 'talents' of the country's new lodgers became ap-parent as bashings and robberies became more prevalent and drunken and boisterous behaviour led to riots. In an effort to stop these, Governor Phillip prohibited the trade of alcohol. It was even forbidden to remove liquor from the ships, but the demand for grog was great and the ease with which seamen could profit made it a greater attraction than Phillip's deterrents.

For those who were caught the punishment was harsh: lashes across the back with the cat-o'-nine-tails or a period on dreaded Pinchgut (now Fort Denison). For those found drunk, similar punishments were given. People began experimenting with the flora in an unsuccessful attempt to find a stimulant. The Governor's order had curtailed many and the supply outlet dropped. With liquor harder to come by and convict appetites insatiable, the demand for illicit grog was high and with it the price; and although the flow slowed, it still continued.

A song indicating the convicts' lust for rum was sung by many:

Cut yer name across me backbone,
Stretch me skin across yer drum,
Iron me up on Pinchgut Island
From now to Kingdom Come.
I'll eat yer Norfolk Dumpling
Like a juicy Spanish plum,
Even dance the Newgate Hornpipe
If ye'll only gimme Rum!

The term 'to dance the Newgate Hornpipe' meant to dance from the gallows, and 'to eat a Norfolk Dumpling' meant to be sent to the notorious Norfolk Island.

The first houses from which grog was dispensed were

The famous Breakfast Creek Hotel, Brisbane, was built in 1889, on the spot where John Oxley is supposed to have landed and had breakfast during the voyage on which he discovered the Brisbane River. A conglomeration of architectural styles, the hotel is one of Brisbane's landmarks.

The Melbourne Hotel in Perth, Western Australia, with its pretty balcony highlighting an interesting facade.

Left: On opposite corners in the isolated mining town of Broken Hill, New South Wales, stand two interesting-looking pubs: the stone Imperial which, with thirty-eight other pubs, was established in 1888, and the Miner's Lamp, which was once the Southern Cross. In 1902 the town boasted over sixty hotels, most of them to help satisfy the miners' thirsts.

The Cosmopolitan Hotel at Carrington, New South Wales, where the State Dockyard's floating dock operated for shipbuilding and where Newcastle's major wharves are located.

Coal was found at the site of Newcastle in 1791 by convicts who escaped from Sydney by boat. Six years later when another group of convicts fled, they were sought by Lieutenant John Shortland who named the river after Governor John Hunter. In 1804 Governor Philip King established a penal settlement at which coal was mined, timber felled and cut, and lime for mortar burnt. Settlers slowly moved into the area in the 1840s and the port grew as more coal was mined and shipped. Steel and heavy industry began and flourished in World War I years. Newcastle is now a major industrial city and one of the country's largest and busiest ports, with coal, wheat, dairy products, iron and steel exports being loaded there.

probably made of canvas. Tents brought out from England were assembled to shelter as many people as possible until more permanent structures could be built. Wattle-and-daub houses, hastily constructed, were followed by the still primitive slab-sided and bark-roofed huts whose walls were packed with mud and clay to stop the weather. From these rough dwellings deals were made, conspiracies conjured and spirits sold. Within a year kilns had been built and bricks were being produced. The forerunners of today's hotels were becoming more stable and elaborate buildings.

Illegal trading and profiteering continued. At the end of 1792, Governor Phillip endeavoured to stop black-market activities by granting the first licence to sell alcohol. Thomas Reibey and Captain Essex Bond from the *Royal Admiral* were allowed to sell their supply of goods and beer, but the problems were not solved. With the arrival of merchant ships seeking easy money it was simple to smuggle alcohol to the ready market.

At the end of 1792, Governor Arthur Phillip left Australia bound for England. A couple of weeks after his departure, the *Hope* arrived carrying a large supply of liquor and food. The captain refused to split the cargo—all had to be bought, or nothing. With a grave food shortage in the colony, Major Grose, the military governor was forced to buy. More than 7000 gallons (almost 32 000 litres) of liquor were purchased at 4s 6d per gallon and offered for a small fee to the military and civil officers, noncommissioned soldiers and seamen.

With the power of alcohol distribution in their hands, some of the military sought easy profits by exploiting the convict and his love for liquor. There was little monetary currency, and liquor became the accepted means of exchange. Land grants were made to officers and Major Grose allowed convicts (in their free time) to hire their labour to these landholders for a payment of rum. Even the Reverend Richard Johnson's church, built in 1793, was partly paid for in rum valued exorbitantly at 10s per gallon after being purchased by Johnson for only 4s 6d per gallon.

As ships arrived, the cargoes were often purchased by military men who sold them at fantastic prices. While Major Francis Grose and his military, the New South Wales Corps, grew fat and rich on easy money, the rest of the community suffered.

A letter written by a soldier in 1794 describes the situation:

> Spirits now being plentiful, a number of persons retail the same, but the price, as well as quality, varies much; the gentlemen always purchase the cargoes, and this watery mixture is sold at 16s per gallon. A convict was not, until very lately, on any account suffered to take spirits in payment for his work, but now the prisoners have plenty of liquor. Liquor, or more properly grog, purchases what money will not, viz., settlers' farms or crops unripe, etc.

Unable to oppose what was virtually a trade monopoly

Amid Sydney's old and new stands the colourful Shelbourne Hotel, which was built in 1902. Busy with plaster patterns, miniature round towers and large walls comprised of arches framing sets of windows, this interesting pub is architecturally important and a wonderful example of the city's Art Nouveau period.

The wonderful old port city of Fremantle, Western Australia, which abounded with pubs in yesteryear to serve the thirsty sailors and men who loaded and unloaded cargoes, looks vibrant and exciting after its restoration for the America's Cup.

After C. Y. O'Connor cleared the mouth of the river and developed an inner safe harbour, the town grew in size and importance and hotels such as the Newcastle Club, built in 1897, were established.

There is no discrimination in the Yanco Glen Hotel, 30 kilometres north of Broken Hill, New South Wales! Here Judy Caldwell, affectionately known as 'the Artistic Swearer', runs a pub full of characters.

Below: *The small town of Ravensthorpe, 190 kilometres west of Esperance, Western Australia, was surveyed in 1848 by A. S. Roe and named by visiting Bishop Short after his parish in Northampton, England. Graziers had taken up most of the good country in the vicinity by 1868 and although prospectors such as George and Tom Stennet had been fossicking in the Ravensthorpe Ranges since 1891, it wasn't until Jim Dunn found alluvial gold and claimed the government reward that the town began to grow. Although goldmining was short-lived, coppermining prospered.*

In 1907 the large two-storey brick Palace Hotel was built, with its scalloped woodwork verandah, its fine stained-glass window and timber staircase. The closure in 1971 of the Ravensthorpe Copper Mine, which had supplied one-third of the State's copper, reduced the town's population.

Above: *On the opal fields of White Cliffs, NSW, where timber is short and thirst is long, stands a miner's home made of beer cans.*

Kangaroo shooters first discovered opal in 1887 and took it to the Wilcannia Survey Office from where it was taken to Germany. Overseas buyers, amid much publicity, visited the isolated area. Diggers flocked to the arid region establishing a population of over 4000 by 1898. Four hotels sprang into existence but town numbers dwindled as opal was discovered at Lightning Ridge in 1909 and Coober Pedy in 1915.

Right: *In the rich farming district of Lismore, New South Wales, stands the three-storey Winsome Hotel. An attractive verandah and balcony grace the original two storeys built in the early 1900s. The top floor was added in 1925.*

backed by the courts, the small farmers and landholders suffered. Those who failed had their land taken over by those who caused their fall. Two years after he had taken office, Major Grose left the colony. William Paterson took the place of Grose, but did little to change the situation.

In February 1794, John Hunter was officially appointed Governor and returned to Sydney in September 1795 to find chaos. The home government had ordered him to control liquor sales and bring about some sort of order. In an endeavour to supervise the quality and quantity of alcohol, restrict the waste of much-needed grain and bring some lawfulness into the grog-oriented settlement, he set to work banishing stills. Any person found breaking this law was to have his or her shanty pulled down as a deterrent to others. To many the risks were worth it and little notice was taken of his orders.

Unable to stamp out the stills, Hunter decided to license a few in the hope that by controlling some a good standard and quality would be assured and people would refuse to buy grog from the backyard brewer. In April 1796 'ten persons were selected by the magistrates, and to them licences for twelve months, under the hands of three magistrates, were granted.' The fee for the annual license was £20, with a £10 surety offered by two persons as a testimony to the character of the licensee. Operating hours were as the licensee saw fit, but opening was forbidden during church hours on Sunday and convicts were not to be sold liquor after 8.00 p.m.

These first public houses were the homes of the licensees, the parlour being used as the bar. The conditions and service offered varied: some were 'bloodhouses'; others, such as that at Parramatta owned by James Larra, pro-vided fine food, good drink and warm hospitality to their customers.

Illicit stills and grog houses flourished. For the number of people, ten legal pubs were too few and more licences were issued in April 1797. One of those to receive a licence was Sarah Bird, who became the first woman in Australia to legally run a public house. These first pubs were generally self-sufficient. Their owners grew vegetables, made their own bread and beer and produced eggs, milk and butter.

Because grog, often nearly poisonous, was still being produced and sold, Hunter tried to encourage the popularity of beer. Anyone was allowed to brew his own. John Boston brewed beer from Indian corn flavoured with the leaves of the love apple (tomato). James Squire, having experimented with the growing of hops at Parramatta, sold his beer in his 'Malting Shovel', and it soon became very popular and famous. On a tombstone at Parramatta an epitaph read:

He who drinks Squire's beer
Lies here.

Squire's own tomb was removed from the old Brickfield Cemetery and taken to one at La Perouse. Part of his tombstone epitaph reported that:

He arrived in the Colony in the First Fleet, and by integrity and Industry acquired an unsullied reputation. Under his care the hop plant was first cultivated in this Settlement, and the first brewery was erected which progressively matured to perfection.

Nearby Hobart's waterfront rests the two-storey brick Alexandra Hotel, known also as the Hope and Anchor. The original pub of 1807 would have differed greatly from this structure with its Doric columns and elaborate brackets supporting a tiny balcony.

were forced to leave their farms and do other work. That was the situation when Philip Gidley King landed in Sydney in April 1800, much to the resentment of Hunter, who was recalled and who sailed out of Sydney at the end of September.

Governor King tried to combat the enormous problems by selling goods directly through government stores and restricting the imports of spirits. In an effort to obtain more respectability and better social behaviour, a Government Order issued in October 1800 forbade licensees to allow drunkenness, disorder or gambling on their property. Liquor was to be sold in exact measures, and could not be served between the beating of the tattoo (around 9.00 p.m.) and noon the following day, and houses had to be closed on Sunday during church services. For those caught breaking the law, a £5 fine was inflicted. As a further attempt to smash the trafficking of illegal brews, permits had to be obtained by anyone transporting more than half a gallon (about 2 litres) of spirits.

Some pubs were appalling places. In his book, *Settlers and Convicts*, Harris described the conditions of a pub typical of many:

> [It was] an old dilapidated place, properly enough called "The Sheer Hulk", which had been deprived of its licence on account of the practices and characters admitted by its landlord; it was, however, still occupied, and as the occupier was no longer under the apprehension of losing his licence, the scenes displayed nightly were of tenfold worse character than ever. So that detection and legal evidence were evaded, all that was cared for by the scoundrel who held it was attained … We found it full to suffocation of the lowest women, sailors, and ruffians, who supported themselves by waylaying and robbing and often murderously wounding any intoxicated sea officer, newly-arrived emigrant, or up-country settler, who might chance to wander into their infernal precinct; and as part of the occupation of the women was to act as lures, of course this was no rare occurence. The door was kept barred, and there was an outlet behind up the rocks … There is no doubt nevertheless that such a nest would have been rooted out

On the Darling Downs at Warwick, 160 kilometres south-west of Brisbane, stands the Universal Hotel. A large timber pub with attractive roofline and balcony, the pub caters for the townsfolk, wheat growers, dairy producers and graziers. There are many fine Victorian buildings contributing to this interesting Queensland town.

Stores were still controlled by the military, some of whom were fleecing the settlers by charging exorbitant prices for goods. As a fairer means of representation, Hunter allowed settlers to choose a number of persons to represent their community in purchasing goods directly from the store ships. This method proved unsuccessful and Hunter had to appoint his own officers to perform the function. Macarthur, the regimental paymaster, and Williamson, the acting commissary, became agents distributing rum and goods and once again the lives of many were controlled by few.

In a country vastly different from England, people found it difficult to survive. Thievings and bashings were common, and civic pride was unknown. The rules of the land were distorted by corrupt opportunists who sought their fortunes at the expense of others. Most of the landholders who had been given grants by Governor Phillip

On the long flag Eyre Highway linking the east with Western Australia is the Nullarbor Hotel, a roadhouse supplying petrol and accommodation for tourists and supply trucks. Here it sits in isolation, surrounded by saltbush, under a vast expanse of sky.

In 1841 explorer Edward John Eyre with John Baxter and three Aborigines set out from Adelaide to cross the treeless plains to Albany. Two of the Aborigines killed Baxter and absconded with the supplies, leaving Wylie and Eyre to perish. They reached Albany on 7 July after an exhausting trip of four and a half months. Western Australian explorer John Forrest traversed the Nullarbor from Perth to Adelaide in 1870. The railway was begun in 1911 and completed in 1917 but most early travellers and gold prospectors followed camel tracks from property to property, as there was no surveyed road from Penong to Norseman until World War I. It wasn't until 1976 that the road was sealed with bitumen.

Top: *In 1888 prospectors Tom Riseley and Mick Toomey, who were told to travel to a row of Western Australian hills just east of the Southern Cross constellation, found gold and a boom followed. To lighten the loads of miners, a pub called the Club was built but was destroyed by fire in 1893 and replaced by the present Club Hotel. At this time the majority of the gold-rush population fled to the Coolgardie fields 240 kilometres east. To speed their journey, Cobb & Co. coaches departed regularly from the pub. The town of Southern Cross survived and in the early 1900s the Club Hotel was headquarters of the Tattersalls Club and the Southern Cross Racing Club.*

Above: *A simple little pub fringed by verandahs, the Collie Hotel at Collie, near Gilgandra, New South Wales, recently burnt down. An establishment known as the Marthagai Inn graced the site from the 1860s. Its name was changed to the Collie Hotel in 1877 and it continued to serve the grazing community and teamsters.*

Left: Kept cool by its large wide verandahs, the Globe Hotel at Barcaldine, Queensland, caters for the thirsts of those in the small town and many workers on surrounding cattle stations. The town emerged in 1886 on Barcaldine Downs, a property then owned by Charles Cameron.

Right: In the garden city of Toowoomba, Queensland, stands the Norville Hotel with its very interesting facade.

Below Left: An interesting roofline and what appears to be an incomplete tower dominates the P&O Hotel, which was built in 1896, in Fremantle, Western Australia. Like so many other city buildings, its verandah has been replaced with an awning.

long before but for the handsome "sweeteners" [bribes] which old D——'s profits enabled him to give the constables. At this time almost every constable in Sydney and indeed in the colony had been a prisoner of the Crown; I believe there were two or three old soldiers in the force, but their principles were not a whit superior, so far as I heard and observed, to those of the convict class. These sly grog shops sold rum only, or rather grog; though, adulterated as it was, it hardly deserved even that name. The trade of the "Sheer Hulk" was often a couple of gallons a night at 1s 3d per half pint, or by gross receipts about 21. Of this 21, it possibly cost old D—— 10s or 12s for rum, a few pence for burnt sugar, the same for tobacco, which together with the water (and some said a dash of vitriol) made up the beverage.

During 1801 and 1802 the French ships, *Géographe* and *Naturaliste*, said to be on scientific searches, were hovering around Van Diemen's Land. Alarmed by the possibility that the French were planning to form a settlement, Governor King wrote to the Secretary of State for Colonies in May 1802 recommending that a British settlement be formed at Port Phillip. Lieutenant-Colonel David Collins was given command of vessels and appointed Lieutenant-Governor of the new colony, his powers being directly under that of King's.

Collins, like King, had little success in controlling the problems caused by grog. Following Hunter's lead, King tried to establish a beer industry. Writing to Governor King in August 1802, Lord Hobart said:

I strongly approve of our continued exertions to prevent the improper importation of spirits. The introduction of beer into general use among the inhabitants would certainly tend in a great degree to lessen the consumption of spirituous liquors; I have therefore, in conformity with your suggestions, taken measures for furnishing the colony, with a supply of ten tons of porter, six bags of hops, and two complete sets of brewing utensils.

As time slid by, beer became more popular and the government established a brewery at Parramatta in September 1804. Under the supervision and knowhow of Thomas Rushton, it at first produced about 1800 gallons (8200 litres) of beer per week; it later increased its output to around 3000 gallons (about 14 000 litres) per week. Farmers, in exchange for ripe barley, wheat or hops, were allowed to purchase 32 gallons (about 145 litres) of beer at 1s 4d per gallon. They had to supply their own casks and guarantee not to sell it for more than 3d per pint.

The liquor situation remained bad. In Tasmania, disorder and corruption were rife. The colony housed the worst of Britain's criminals, and prostitutes and scoundrels were placed as hotelkeepers. Records of Tasmania's first taverns and inns have not been found but from letters describing the settlements they appear to have been filthy squalid shacks in which adulterated grog was dispensed at considerable profit by unsavoury people. Governor King had ordered Collins to fine the owners and confiscate the liquor of those unlicensed houses, but most authorities were as crooked as the convicts and control was impossible. Things changed when the 1805 famine prevented food being used for alcohol. Many houses and breweries closed but this temporary control did not last long, for when the famine ended the situation reverted to the same unruly conditions as before.

The government-owned brewery at Parramatta, while profitable when it began, was now running at a loss. In February 1806 the government leased the business to Rushton who quickly made it a profitable brewery, selling strong beer for 1s a gallon and table beer for 6d a gallon. About the same time a private brewery was started in Sydney by P. Larken.

Governor King had reduced the exploitation of convict labour employed by the military and in trying to smash their power had made many enemies. In England, after hearing only the evidence from John Macarthur (who was facing court martial) and reading letters from those opposed to King, Whitehall dispatched a letter to the Governor granting him permission for the retirement he sought. William Bligh arrived in August 1806, and took over the control of the colony six days later.

Bligh was horrified at the situation confronting him and astounded by the power wielded by those with a supply of spirits. As payment in rum was worth far more than its equivalent value in money or anything else, the military, who controlled its flow, had monopolistic powers. Bligh instructed that no spirits were allowed to be landed in the colony without his consent and the military were no longer to trade in alcohol.

In February 1807 Bligh issued a general order prohibiting the exchange of spirits or other liquors as payment for food, grain, labour, clothes or other commodities. If disobeyed, the penalties were severe: a convict was liable to a hundred lashes and twelve months' hard labour: an emancipist could receive up to three months' hard labour, a £20 fine and loss of all indulgences from the Crown; free settlers were imposed with a fine of £50 and the loss of all privileges. To those who informed on the lawbreaker, a reward of half the amount of the fine was given.

It was easy to prohibit liquor trading, but the civil and criminal courts were controlled by the military. Realising he must break this obstacle in order to administer his law effectually, Bligh asked London to appoint an independent attorney-general and judge.

In the same year a cargo ship arrived carrying a 40-gallon (182-litre) still for Captain Edward Abbott, of the New South Wales Corps, and a 60-gallon (273-litre) still for John Macarthur. Bligh, having prohibited the distillation of spirits, ordered that they be placed in government stores until they could be shipped back. The head and worm of the 60-gallon still had been removed to make the product unusable for its purpose, and the copper container was given to Macarthur. In October, when a ship was ready to sail for England, Bligh ordered both complete stills be loaded. When fronted for collection, Macarthur demanded a receipt. Written on this was 'two stills with heads and worms'. Macarthur rejected this on the grounds that the heads and worms had never been in his

The Birdsville pub rings with excitement and good cheer as thousands of people, dogs, horses, cars and aircraft inundate the tiny border town for the annual picnic races.

Augustus Poeppel, while surveying the Queensland–South Australian border in 1879, established a camp he named Diamantina Crossing. When construction of the border fence began in 1883, station owner Robert Frew renamed it Birdsville after the prolific birdlife and established the first pub and store to cater for the needs of stationhands, drovers and fence builders.

Built in 1884 of local stone topped by a corrugated-iron roof, the Birdsville Hotel played an important part in serving the needs of isolated stations, the customs post and police station, and is now the town's only licensed pub, the Tattersalls having closed in 1915 followed by the Royal in 1925.

Quorn, situated in the remarkable South Australian Flinders Ranges, has become a haven for tourists and rail enthusiasts. Old steam locomotives are kept running by volunteers who operate them from Quorn through the famous Pitchi Ritchi Pass. The town, built mainly of stone, was established in 1875 and blossomed after the railway was built. Wheat was grown (before the long line of droughts proved this a mistake) and flour milled locally. The Great Junction Hotel and three other hotels were built in the 1880s, the railway carrying the clientele to fill their beds.

Dwarfed by Perth's modern skyscrapers, the opulent Palace Hotel stands as a reminder of the wealth of the gold rush days and elegance of a bygone era. This grand hotel was built in 1895 by an adventurer, John De Baun. An energetic man, he was one of many Americans who flocked to the Australian goldfields.

From the Ballarat, Victoria, goldfields he tried his hand jackarooing at Wilcannia, New South Wales, before finding gold at nearby Silverton and establishing a pub. When it burnt down he built the Grand Hotel in Broken Hill. From there he ventured to Adelaide where he lost his fortune in the 1890s Depression. At Coolgardie on Western Australia's goldfields he 'struck it rich' and went to Perth, bought land originally granted to William Leeder and spent £64 000 building an opulent Victorian three-storey hotel designed by architects Porter and Thomas.

Sparing no cost, its bricks were shipped from Melbourne, cedar for the staircase and panelling was brought from New South Wales and marble for the fireplaces was imported from Italy. It housed a post and telegraph office, a library, a reading room, a smoking room, 130 bedrooms, 12 bathrooms with hot and cold water on tap, a billiard room, 5 wine cellars, dining rooms, drawing rooms, beautiful cedar-lined bars, and stables. It boasted fresh daily produce from its own farms. Unfortunately, in the name of progress, it has recently been closed, its interiors gutted, and it is now used as office space.

possession. When Robert Campbell Jnr collected it, Macarthur brought action against him for illegal seizure of property. A bench of magistrates comprising Major Johnston, Commissary John Palmer, and Advocate Atkins gave victory to Macarthur.

Squabbles between Bligh and Macarthur continued. On their return from Tahiti in November 1807 the crew of the *Parramatta*, owned by Macarthur and Hullets Brothers, declared they had smuggled a notorious convict from Sydney. Bligh took action and seized the ship. One incident led to another and before long Johnston had consulted with officers and assumed the title of Lieutenant-Governor. Bligh was arrested in January 1808. This battle for power was appropriately labelled the Rum Rebellion!

Following the dismissal of Bligh's supporters from public office, corruption reigned. In July 1808 Lieutenant-Colonel Joseph Foveaux, Johnston's senior officer, returned from four years in England and assumed leadership. The situation worsened. Paterson, in Van Diemen's Land, had ignored the situation until 1809 when he arrived in Sydney to take charge. Little changed. Bligh was eventually released from prison on the condition that he would leave Australia, and Johnston was ordered to return to England to offer reason for his actions. Meanwhile Paterson, who had become Foveaux's puppet, granted land to officers and men of the New South Wales Corps and grog flowed freely once more. John Jamison wrote:

> [the officers] obtain Spirits to what Amount they please, which they sell from five Hundred to a Thousand per cent for Grain to the unthinking Settlers who have been deprived from procuring a single Drop by any other Channel, since the unfortunate day of the unjust Arrest of His Excellency Governor Bligh.

Governor Lachlan Macquarie, who succeeded Bligh, had been ordered to establish authority, promote confidence and produce a law abiding state. No spirits were to be landed without his permission, and alcohol was not to be used as a monetary article. By order of the King, he announced that all authorisations made by the rebel government were to be annulled. This included land grants, pardons and punishments. Those who had lost their positions because of Bligh's deposal were to be reappointed. To enforce his laws, Macquarie had brought with him the 73rd Regiment, which replaced the New South Wales Corps.

The whole structure of the colony revolved around alcohol. Macquarie set out first to reduce the number of public house licences. He suggested twenty for Sydney, four for Parramatta, six for the Hawkesbury region, one for the inn on the road between Sydney and the Hawkesbury, and another for the halfway house between Parramatta and Sydney. He decided also to issue licences for the sale of beer, and in July 1810 Judge-Advocate Ellis Bent granted fifty. Imposed was a £5 fee and £25 surety. The rules were the same as for those holding licences for the sale of spirits, except that the beer retailers were not permitted to sell spirits.

The arched carriageway is a particularly attractive feature of the old red brick store/barracks which stands behind the Clarendon Arms Hotel at Evandale, Tasmania. An integral part of the charming village, the inn was built in 1847.

Two beautifully crafted lamps hang over the doorway of the Clarendon Arms.

Seeing the way to obtain a much-needed public building at very little cost, Macquarie, in 1810, let the contract for the construction of a hospital to Garnham Blaxcell, Alexander Riley and D'Arcy Wentworth. The agreement was that the government would supply them with convict labour, food and twenty oxen to help with the building, and they were to construct the hospital at their expense for the right to import 45 000 gallons (about 205 000 litres) of Bengal Rum over a three-year period. In this way Macquarie made use of the 'rum fever' to benefit the colony.

As a further means of control, licences for commercial breweries were introduced in 1811. The four that were granted licenses were owned by Absalom West and Thomas Rushton, both of Sydney, Henry Kable of Windsor and James Squire of Kissing Point. To clamp down further on illicit sellers and producers, liquor was not allowed to be moved without the permission of the authorities. However, corruption was great and police and citizens turned a blind eye as they were invariably involved themselves. No-one was allowed to import spirits and the official level of importation dropped drastically from 77 355 gallons (about 352 000 litres) in 1811 to 29 807 gallons (135 500 litres) the following year. The result was a notable increase in smuggling and home brewing.

When he realised that he could not stop private distillers, Macquarie changed his tactics. A Government Order issued at the end of 1814 allowed the importation of spirits to Sydney, Hobart and Port Dalrymple. Macquarie applied a large duty and hoped that by creating competition a more realistic price and quality of liquor might be obtained.

Because rum was an inflationary currency, he reduced its value by giving Australia its own coinage. The centres of Spanish coins were punched out: the outer part was referred to as the 'holey dollar' and the inner as the 'dump'. It was the first time the country had had its own legal tender, and meant that a fair and consistent price system could be fixed. About the same time, England instructed

Wearing its large identifying sign, the Queen's Arms Hotel at the small town of Springsure is a welcome sight on a hot day.

Located 300 kilometres to the west of Rockhampton, Queensland, Springsure rests in a lee surrounded by beautiful craggy rugged peaks of old volcanoes down which water is fed to springs. Graziers, wheat growers and their employees are the hotel's regular customers.

In 1842 Henry Russell and Captain Joliffe sailed up the Mary River and settled on land for woolgrowing at Tiaro, near Maryborough, Queensland. Sheep and supplies were sailed in but hostile Aborigines and disease caused the venture to fail. The Hideaway Hotel near Tiaro station is tucked off the main road.

Although the ground floor of the Crown and Sceptre Hotel has been barbarically altered and its verandah removed, the original upper facade remains. The hotel was constructed by the one-time Northern Territory surveyor and Overland Telegraph inspector William McMinn. In the 1870s he built a series of lovely terraces, hotels and the Supreme Court, which added elegance to North Terrace, Adelaide.

that the traditional supply of spirits from public stores to officials was to stop.

In 1815 licences for the sale of beer only were stopped. A year later brewers were forbidden to retail alcohol, which resulted in the producers establishing and supplying their own hotels. Public houses serving spirits were obliged to obtain beer licences and, for those refusing to serve beer, a £10 fine was imposed. By applying these regulations, a person was no longer restricted to certain public houses because of what he drank, but was free to drink where he wished. Fifty of these licenses (whose fee increased to £30) were issued for Sydney, six for Parramatta, four for Windsor, one for Liverpool and three for roadhouses. Shortly after this system came into operation, brewers declared their trade was suffering, so twenty beer licenses for Sydney, eight for Parramatta and four for Windsor were issued at a fee of £5.

At last the colony was showing signs of success. Good roads had been built, allowing faster travel, and the traveller was offered good accommodation in fine inns. Building techniques and materials had improved, giving inns and public houses a vastly different image from the earlier establishments. Service had improved, and food and drink were generally of a good standard.

Public houses had colourful names, such as these listed in the *Sydney Gazette* in 1817:

Green Man, Rose, Cherry Tree, Saint Patrick, Red Lion, Cat and Fiddle, Governor King, Bunch of Grapes, Feathers, Bull's Head, King George, Labour in Vain, Crown and Thistle, Blacksmith's Arms, Dog and Duck, Foul Anchor, King's Arms, King's Head, Windmill, Hope and Anchor, Punch Bowl, Speed the Plough, Bee Hive, Duke of Wellington, Greyhound, Adam and Eve, Saint George, Westmoreland Arms, Pine Apple, Black Swan, New Zealander, Horse and Jockey, Golden Fleece, Green Gate, Blue Lion, Lord Nelson, Robin Hood, Saint Paul's, Unicorn, Grapes, Chelsea Pensioner, Good Woman, Lord Nelson's Victory, Pot of Beer, Freemason's Arms, Thatched House, Hawkesbury Settler, Red Cow, Bird in Hand, the Struggler, Rose and Crown, Glasgow Arms, Elizabeth Powell's Half-way House to Parramatta, Macquarie Arms, Royal Oak, Crooked Billet, the Hope, William Roberts' Half-way House to Liverpool, First and Last.

In many cases the same name was given to a number of

The charming old Peninsula Hotel at Mandurah overlooks the mouth of Peel Inlet into which the waters of the Harvey, Serpentine and Murray Rivers enter. The name Mandurah is derived from an Aboriginal word 'wandjar' meaning 'trading place'. Fishing in the beautiful estuary is popular with locals and the many tourists who venture the 60 kilometres south from Perth.

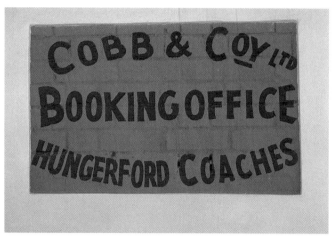

The old Cobb & Co. booking office sign on the wall of the Carrier's Arms Hotel, which was licensed in 1876. The Carrier's Arms is in Bourke, New South Wales.

style. In New South Wales, with its hot days and heavy rainfall, the verandah became a feature; in Tasmania, hotels and climate resembled those of England.

In addition to the charming and simple inns that arose, and the practical and well-packed public houses and taverns, a number of beautiful and grand hotels had been built. Georgian in design, they made use of the fine local cedar, improved technology and materials and craftsmanship that were now more easily imported.

By the time Macquarie left Australia standards had risen, the economy had greater stability and there were many fine buildings. Few illicit liquor producers or sly-grog sellers operated. Australia had established a comparatively sophisticated image.

Officials in England were somewhat unhappy at the leniency Macquarie had displayed in his dealings with convicts. The Secretary of State for Colonies expressed the view that Australia's image should be one of a harsh penal

pubs. At others, no name was given and the hotel or inn was known by the name of its licensee.

In Tasmania, licensed taverns and inns were fewer in number but displayed similar names. The Whale Fishery had received its licence in 1807, and the Hope, and Derwent Tavern were legally recognised the following year. Other pubs to be licensed were the Union, Plough, Carpenter's Arms, Dusty Miller, Bricklayer's Arms, Bird in Hand, Cat and Fiddle, New Inn, City of London Arms and Calcutta. Many of the waterfront pubs were sources for recruiting crews for whaling ships.

The pub names illustrate the feelings of the times. One can visualise their colourfully painted swinging signs; or imagine the noise of hearty laughter, the rowdy rebukes and boisterous songs being sung; smell the odour of seamen, farmers and builders mingled with the strong aroma of tobacco, the scent of spirits laced with arak and the perfume plastered on the whores. Their character and furnishings were as crude as their customers and the buildings themselves were rough, raw and practical, but providing what was demanded of them.

At this time the public house catered for two types of people and had two standards of service. For the overnight traveller or resident guest a private drinking parlour, usually the landlord's own sitting room, was provided. Meals were taken with the family, and the traveller was given the courtesies of a guest rather than a paying lodger. For the public drinkers, few amenities were provided. The bar room usually consisted of a barely furnished room of little comfort. It was practical but unimaginative, basic and charmless. The liquor was housed in a small adjoining room which came to be known as the taproom. From this, dispensed alcohol was generally passed through a small opening. When the landlord left to attend his boarding guests or family, he locked the taproom door.

The architecture of these buildings differed from area to area. Climate, location, materials obtainable, money available, craftsmen and builders, density of population and fashions of the time had an influence on each pub's

Export lager on tap with dunnies nearby. Coolgardie, Western Australia, has now only one licensed hotel, the Denver City, built in 1897–98 during the gold rush. Still standing but no longer trading are the Ghost Inn (formerly the Railway Hotel), the Marble Bar built 1898–1900, and the skeleton of the White Hart.

Above: *On highway 31, between Yass and Gundagai, NSW, the St George Tavern at Jugiong has long been a favourite stop for truckies.*

Below: *On a cold winter's night a drop of port is much appreciated.*

settlement. This, he reasoned, would discourage more people from breaking English laws. Colonel Arthur followed his recommendations and governed Tasmania with a tight rein. In one case he refused to issue a new licence to Thomas Ransom of the Joiner's Arms Hotel because he wasn't married to the woman with whom he lived.

In 1823 under the rule of Governor Brisbane, an Act allowed an advisory Legislative Council and a Supreme Court of New South Wales to be established. This, to some degree, shifted the load of power and responsibility. More people with capital to invest were migrating or sending their money, and with more influence than convicts, they sought to have their views heard. Rules regarding alcohol control set by previous governors were made law in an Act in 1825. Pubs were obliged to close at 9.00 p.m. and remain closed on Sundays. A year later another Act restricted convicts' drinking time to 8.00 p.m. and legalised the Governor's right to specify the number of licences at any time. Previously, recommendations made by the Governor were often ignored by the licensing magistrates.

To improve the standards of public houses, orders were introduced demanding that accommodation of reasonable standards be provided when required. Sitting rooms had to be available and good meals given if wanted. A sign showing the proprietor's name had to be openly displayed above the door, over which a lamp to light the public street at night had to hang. These demands involved considerable expense for many publicans, and forced higher standards and improved conditions in most hotels. Those taverns and inns whose owners were unwilling to comply with the regulations were forced to close.

Some hotels offered fine rooms at reasonable tariffs but others, while remaining within the law, provided only cramped rough dormitory conditions. This was rectified by an Act stipulating that rooms had to be of moderate sizes.

Until 1833 hotels had been establishments that sold general products as well as liquor. A new Act passed by the courts prohibited pubs from selling anything other than liquor and meals and shops from selling alcohol in smaller quantities than bottles.

Explorers were opening up more areas and in their tracks the inns followed. The services they offered varied according to the host, but there was a marked difference between them and the public houses of the large established port settlements. Constructed of local materials, the inns were usually narrow single-storey buildings with a verandah slung from at least one side. They were often set within a garden of cool trees, colourful flowers and much-needed vegetables. Stables, and often a coach-house, stood at the rear of the inn.

From the early years, governors realised the necessity of the inn as a provider of accommodation and meals for the traveller and his horse. This became far more evident when coach travel was introduced and more people were in need of hospitality and shelter. At a halfway house the weary traveller could recuperate in a homely atmosphere or take refreshments while a fresh team was being harnessed.

As more land was needed and farmers set off in search of better pastures for their starving flocks and herds, the remote inns were welcome sights. These pioneer buildings provided immeasurable service to those who followed and settled. As more people came to live in the area, a store would emerge to cater for their needs. A blacksmith would follow, perhaps another store, a few more farmers and in a short time a small community or town would have mushroomed. A little later and another inn would have emerged to cater for those travelling between towns.

The innkeeper generally ran a number of businesses. In many isolated places he was a mailman, storekeeper, blacksmith, farmer, lawman, newsman, punt-operator and

Left top: The beer garden at the Watsons Bay Hotel overlooks Sydney's spectacular harbour into the city centre. There were once five hotels in the district, now only one remains.

Left middle: A substantial waterhole (the Nungarin Hotel) marks the railway siding from which wheat is railed. Nungarin is just north of Merredin, halfway between Kalgoorlie and Perth.

Merredin, with its permanent waterhole and shanty, became the stopping place for diggers on their way to the eastern goldfields. After the railway opened in 1893, it become a junction and centre for local grazing and wheat-growing industries.

Left: Near Brisbane's Roma Street Station, the Transcontinental Hotel is overshadowed by the city's skyscrapers. Built in 1884, the hotel has been tastefully restored and caters for the bustling city workers.

The Hexham Hotel at Hexham, 70 kilometres north of Warrnambool, Victoria, was formerly the Woolshed Inn. It was sold in 1854 by a Mr Kennedy to William Brunsley who erected this substantial bluestone hotel. Sheep producers and shearers are the pub's main clients.

stock agent, as well as a provider of good simple food, accommodation and warm companionship.

Higher standards were being demanded by the public. Buildings were being constructed with greater attention to detail and to the customers' needs. Baths with hot and cold water, billiard tables, drawing rooms, better furnishings and decorations were being added as enticements to attract patronage. Taprooms had become storerooms, and bar counters were common in most pubs.

One of the biggest influences on the style of many pubs was the Building Act of 1837, which came into effect at the beginning of 1838. Derived from the 1780 London Building Act, it ruled that no windows, roofline or any other structures were to project past the street face; no timber building was to be constructed for fear of fire, and specified regulations for fireplaces and chimneys had to be met; dividing and external walls of stone or brick had to be a specific thickness and timber doors and windows were required to be recessed a minimum of 4 inches (10 centimetres).

There was much opposition to the Building Act. Builders and architects argued that the climate necessitated a verandah or roof extension for protection from rain and sun. Officials set up a panel to study the matter, and this resulted in an amendment to the Act being passed in October 1838. Verandahs made of hardwood were allowed to be built provided that they adjoined a brick or stone wall at least 9 inches (23 centimetres) thick; iron or stone balconies were permitted to overlap the footpath by 38 inches (96 centimetres). There was still much opposition but the law remained in force until 1879.

In order to dissuade other countries from claiming land, the British Government realised that settlements would have to be formed along parts of Australia's coast. Free settlers, officials and some soldiers, under the authority of Captain James Stirling, sailed from England bound for Perth, a settlement to which no convicts were to be sent.

Undoubtedly, the hoped-for success of the newly proclaimed Colony of Western Australia was sealed and resealed by alcoholic toasts. Only five and a half months later, on the first day of 1830, a special licensing committee issued licences for the sale of wine, ale and beer. At Perth, the Swan, Perth and Happy Emigrant Hotels were issued licences; the South Sea Hall, Collins', Stirling Arms and George IV Hotels, all at Freemantle, were also licensed. These hotels and inns were similar in design, character and requirements to Sydney's early ones. They were obliged to close at 10.00 p.m., encourage respectable customers, prevent gambling, and abstain from tampering with the drinks or using grog as a means of exchange.

The number of inns and public houses was found to be too few, and more licences were issued during the year. From then on, as the population grew or as areas opened up, an inn or hotel would spring into service. Farmers grew barley and brewed their own beer, and by 1833 Burgess Brothers were brewing beer for public consumption. There was far less trouble in the Western Australia colony than there had been in Sydney's penal settlement, and as the people began to prosper, the hotel business swelled.

As explorers made known their finds, pioneers (among them publicans and innkeepers) soon moved into the new territories. John Pascoe Fawkner, who had hotel interests in Tasmania, was one of those who established shanties in Port Phillip, Victoria. At this time the area was a lawbreakers' paradise. Police-Magistrate Lonsdale was sent down to keep order, but he soon realised it was impossible to eradicate the well-established grog-sellers. At the end of October 1836 he gave certificates permitting the sale of liquor in Port Phillip to Michael Carr of the Governor Bourke Hotel, George Smith of the Port Phillip Hotel and Oliver Adams of the Crown Hotel. The following year magistrates had authority to issue licences and more were granted.

Melbourne's population increased substantially, and so did the number of licensed public houses and inns. In 1839, the *Melbourne Advertiser* was published in Fawkner's hotel, which also provided the services of a lending library. The Pavilion in the Eagle Tavern operated as the

An attractive relaxed atmosphere has been created in the recently restored Esplanade Hotel at Fremantle, Western Australia.

34

Above: *The restored Esplanade Hotel was a popular meeting place during the 1987 America's Cup in Fremantle, Western Australia. With lovely long verandahs surmounted by a corner turret, the hotel was designed by J. H. Eagles and built in 1897.*

Below: *A rare storm has dampened the dust in front of the Kingoonya Hotel at Kingoonya, South Australia. Lying north of Lake Harris and 150 kilometres west of Woomera, Kingoonya sits beside the railway which crosses the Nullarbor Plain.*

Cornish miners, affectionately known as 'Cousin Jacks', were attracted in great numbers to South Australia when silver-lead was discovered in 1841 at Glen Osmond and the Burra Burra Copper Mine was established in 1845. In 1861 valuable tracts of copper were found at Moonta, on the coast of Yorke Peninsula south of Port Pirie, and many more Cornish miners flooded to the area following the great copper crash in Cornwall.

To cater for the thirsts of these miners, the Cornwall Hotel, originally known as the Globe, was first licensed in 1865 and, like other pubs in the town, promoted wrestling matches each Christmas and Easter.

Moonta today, with its small neat functional cottages and mining relics, is a popular place for tourists.

first of Melbourne's theatres. The town was really striding forth and, to cater for the many houses legally selling liquor, Mill's brewery and one owned by Murphy were kept busy.

South Australia's first governor was John Hindmarsh. He wanted Adelaide to grow as a community-minded centre catering fairly for the needs of its settlers. Pubs of course, were one of those needs. The early hotels and inns were simple but practical constructions. The first to be licensed, in May 1873, was Guthrie's Hotel, owned by George Guthrie. A month later another four received licences, and the numbers continued to grow. Theatres had been introduced—the first was in the plush Adelaide Tavern. As facilities and industries were established in the growing community, the hotels became more substantial buildings and offered more to the drinkers and travellers.

Brisbane, which grew from the penal settlement of Moreton Bay established in 1824, remained a veritable gaol until free settlers were allowed to build in 1842. No time was wasted in issuing the first licence to Robert Rowland of the Brisbane Hotel. Pubs sprang up to cater for the increasing numbers of people. Their designs were different from those of the other colonies; they were made

A difference in spirits! Launceston's Cornwall Hotel in Tasmania has a historic link with the founding of Melbourne. The original hotel (of which only a small rear section now stands) was built in 1823 by John Pascoe Fawkner. Fawkner was a very enterprising man—he operated a bakery, a nursery and the Launceston Advertiser, *gave lessons in French, pleaded in court when lawyers were in short supply, was a moneylender and operated a coach run*

to Perth (Tasmania) and Longford. His hotel was stocked with a fine library and reading room and it was here that meetings took place with John Batman to plan to cross Bass Strait and form a settlement. J. E. Cox, a mail contractor, purchased the pub in 1832 and established it as a stage coach and goods depot. Fawkner left Launceston to live in Melbourne in 1835.

One of Western Australia's oldest existing hotels, the Rose and Crown at Guildford, a suburb of Perth, was built in 1841. In the cellar is a brick well still in use. Behind the hotel stand the stables used to shelter the horses and camels of guests. The whole complex has been lovingly restored by Lyn and Kemp Hall who have also built one of the country's finest museums, housing the largest private collection in the southern hemisphere.

The old lamp still hangs on the two-storey Georgian Wilmot Arms Inn at Kempton, 50 kilometres north of Hobart. The region was first settled as Green Ponds in 1814 and was renamed after settler Anthony Fenn Kemp who opposed Governor Bligh in the Rum Rebellion of 1808.

of timber, and most had large airy verandahs and stood on stilts. Gardens and verandahs were the coolest places in which to drink, and considerable individuality developed.

The country as a whole was prospering, and people were demanding better conditions in the hotels. Two-storey buildings proved less economical than those with three, four or five storeys that were now being constructed. Sandstone had become fashionable; those who built in brick often plastered the walls and coated them with paint. Attention to detail was far less fastidious than when the earlier grand hotels had been built, but glass, marble, tiles and good furniture were more easily imported. Competition among hotels was fierce, and money and effort were spent by hotelkeepers to make their establishments more attractive and their advertising more distinctive.

Then, between 1840 and 1843, the cancer of economic depression ate into the community and many pubs were forced to close. When business again began to prosper, more and better hotels were built and competition between them became intense. Some publicans provided entertainment in the form of plays, concerts, billiards, skittles, darts, music (often accompanied by sing-songs) and other novelties. Fighting contests among dogs, rats, cocks and men were popular in some pubs. Decor improved, paintings were added and displays were shown. Gardens, in which one could partake of refreshments, were fashionable. Improved technology resulted in structural changes and new appliances. Some hotels even had their own specially made currency, for trade tokens made their appearance about this time.

When the rural economy was flourishing, the 'cockies' and their families visited the cities. They indulged in the services and comforts of lavishly appointed, fashionable hotels that provided entertainment and facilities unprocurable in country areas. When their whims had been satisfied and their business completed, they parted with a handsome wad of notes and returned to their properties.

The 'bushies' also liked to be tempted by the trappings of the gay city life. Having worked long hours under harsh conditions, many would collect their yearly salary and blow into town. They were the target of cardsharps, tricksters, swindlers, bashers and 'ladies', who tried to separate them from their money. In one enormous spree, they and their newly acquired 'friends' would carouse and drink their way through their hard-earned money until, with nothing but a hangover and pleasant memories, they would return to the bush for another year of hard work. Of such people Garryowen's *Chronicles of Melbourne* says: 'These fellows worked harder than horses in the bush, and spent their money like asses in the town.'

Not all bushmen went to the cities to spend their money. Many handed their cheques to landlords of simple country pubs and asked to 'work it off'. When the value of these cheques or the amount stipulated had been consumed in booze, they were sobered up and sent on their way. The habit was known as 'lambing down'.

Transport between major coastal towns was usually carried on by ship, and hence few inns were found between them. Inland settlements, on the other hand, were joined by paths dotted with inns at intervals of a half-day horse or coach ride. Newly formed towns rapidly established inns and public houses, which were often licensed in the operator's wife's name. However, it wasn't until gold was found that the population began to surge inland. Shanty towns sprang up overnight and among them bush pubs and grog houses flourished.

Gold! The news was electrifying and the frenzy of excitement spread like a fanned fire as thousands of people flocked to the fields. Tradesmen, labourers and professional men left their work in the towns and farms, lured by the gold and the prospect (a gamble) of becoming rich. Merchants saw the glint of wealth and transported basic commodities to the areas. People from many different countries and cultures poured into the new El Dorado.

As the cities emptied, the roads were flooded with those seeking their fortunes. Bullock teams carrying supplies of food, tents, tools, alcohol, etc., were relayed to the fast-growing centres. Coach runs became regular and men walked, rode and drove to towns that were springing up overnight. Inns and hotels were built along the way and prices for everything rose.

The fields themselves were colourful but generally crude. Tents, mineshafts and windlasses dotted the countryside. In their midst were the trade buildings. Made of any available material, the conglomeration of buildings resulted in an originality of design and artwork. Some of the bigger and more prosperous centres had inns, hotels, stores, butchers, bakers, churches, police barracks, banks, laundries, baths and courthouses, as well as accommodation a little more comfortable than in the lean-tos or tents.

The hotels at the fields varied. Logs, galvanised iron, bark, tea-tree, timber, pisé, canvas and (later) bricks were used in their construction. The early hotels were primitive and offered little else but grog, shared-bed accommodation and meals. Many bars were dirty, dangerous, hard-pushed places where people from all walks of life drank to celebrate their finds, drown their sorrows or partake in their only social activity.

As more gold was found some pubs improved in stature, furnishings, entertainment, accommodation and service. Concerts were given, music was played, songs were sung, skittles and billiards introduced, gold was bought and alcohol drunk. They were places where fights broke out and laughter was constant; where many different accents and languages were heard. Within the pub walls miners could escape the dry dirty dust or the wet clay and mud. Diseases in the areas were prolific and uncontaminated water was often difficult to obtain. But alcohol flowed freely, and breweries flourished.

Those who found gold shared their good fortune by shouting a glass or two for all. The fever created by the lust for gold led to riots, thefts, murders, bashings, fires and disturbances, all of which were aggravated by the much-dispensed liquor. Things were so bad that in October 1851 hotels were banned from the goldfields and remained so for a number of years. But alcohol was in

Decorative lace adds charm and balance to Ballarat's Golden City Hotel. On freehold land which became available in 1853, the Adelphi was built in 1856. It witnessed the great wealth and booms of the gold rush which is why its owner Dr Robert Hudson changed its name to the Golden City Hotel in 1897. It has recently undergone extensive renovations and is licensed for 302 guests. The balcony has been opened up for the public to enjoy fine foods and wine.

Huge Queensland brick pubs with wide rambling timber verandahs, the Royal and the School of Arts are two of Roma's finest and most dominating buildings. Replacing a magnificent timber hotel which burnt in 1918, the Royal experienced fire in 1926 and the displeasure of a client who shot the hotelier. The School of Arts Hotel was built in 1918 and is reputed to have had the town brothel over its kitchen. Its bar closed early if twelve kegs had been consumed—thirteen was unlucky in one day.

In the 1960s the Western Star published an article about a rich Argentinian horse buyer coming to the School of Arts to buy equines. At the appointed hour red carpet was laid out and poles roped off. At the front door stopped a limousine out of which stepped a dark man dressed in a gold-studded suit with red cummerbund. Two men carrying briefcases and four consorts followed him through the bar. Farmers and riders from the district were dressed 'to the nines' and ready to do business. The man walked straight out the back door and disappeared. The day was 1 April. 'Easter in the Country' is celebrated by a goat race down the main street—$500 to the owner of the first goat past the pub.

Formerly the Burgoyne, the Grand Hotel at Yarra Glen near
Healesville, Victoria, was built by Mr W. C. Farrell, who in 1881
had leased the Yarra Flats Hotel and established a mail coach run.
To gain a licence for his newly proposed hotel, Farrell bought a
condemned pub at Christmas Hills and transferred its licence to the
Burgoyne, which was erected by builders Boyd and Sons in 1888.
Three years after the hotel's foundations had settled, the fourth
storey was added to complete the architectural plans of Gerald Van
Heems. Only three families have owned the hotel: Farrell
1888–1912, Gedye 1912–32 and Lithgow 1932 to present.

In the flat wide dusty country, 70 kilometres along the Barrier
Highway west of the South Australian–New South Wales border,
rests Olary, its pub its most prized possession. Beside the Broken
Hill–Port Pirie railway line, Olary is a major producer of feldspar
for the domestic market.

great demand in this unnatural and compact society, and sly-grog sellers began supplying the thirsty miners. Police often ignored the situation, which was aggravated by the ease with which grog sellers could obtain wholesale licenses.

In most of the towns among the goldfields little planning had occurred during the boom period. If buildings needed to be larger, another section was tacked on. Consequently, each town developed a style of its own, though the verandah was generally a feature of most.

As new finds took a downward turn, many disillusioned miners headed back to the cities and their farms. There was little accommodation available for the numerous immigrants and former goldseekers, so large hotels were hastily constructed on almost every town corner. Architects were kept busy and architecture was influenced by the stream of newly arrived immigrants.

New railway lines were linking more and more towns, and the building industry boomed. Stations were built and near them were erected large hotels with attractive amenities to entice the train traveller to an overnight stay. Commercial travellers and the adventurous began to use this much faster and more comfortable mode of transport. Road travel became less popular and the inns along roads competing with the railway found business slow.

Although large numbers of train travellers generally needed to be fed and housed overnight, competition between hotels was great, and brewers were often invited to stock the bars. This was the start of the tied-house system. Gradually the brewers began to have a tighter control over some pubs until they eventually owned them. Up until then, the hotel had been owned and run by the family, but now individuals and syndicates were obtaining chains of hotels and hiring managers to run them.

As technology and working conditions improved, the worker was given more free time—and drinking in pubs occupied much of it. More drinking rooms were provided, and private bars were introduced into city hotels. These were comfortably appointed rooms let by a number of ladies who would entertain male customers. Liquor, when requested, was sent up from the public bar—but was far more expensive!

Elaborate grand hotels, incorporating all the latest features, were expensively and tastefully furnished and were staffed by well-groomed experienced people. Women were invited to take part in various functions and a separate ladies' lounge protected them from raucous or predatory male customers.

The use of iron, better building techniques and the introduction of elevators allowed hotels to be built higher. Most city pubs, with the exception of Brisbane hotels, no longer had verandahs. Country town hotels were designed sensibly to reduce the effects of uncomfortable climatic conditions. In cold areas rooms were small but had large open fireplaces; the external walls were usually brick or stone, and verandahs were seldom seen. In the hotter areas, verandahs, protected by shady trees, acted as shelters from the weather and were used as drinking areas; balconies, latticed or with iron railings, allowed air

Top: *The large imposing Kurri Kurri Hotel was built in 1904 by Tooheys to serve the coalminers from the twenty-odd mines surrounding the Hunter Valley town of Kurri Kurri, New South Wales. In the early days all mining was done by hand with horses used to pull the skip. Each man had to fill his dag (10 tonnes a shift). Starting at 7.00 a.m. some good miners in ideal conditions (soft coal, safe roof) could fly through their quota and be at the pub by 1.00 p.m. drinking schooners of black beer. Until the late 1950s four bookmakers, and their 'cockatoos' and 'pencillers', fielded on Saturday's Sydney, Melbourne and Brisbane races, their boards set up at the back of the pub. Coalminers and workers from the Alcan smelters continue to quench their thirsts.*

Above: *The quaint Moorine Rock Hotel situated on the Great Eastern Highway just west of Southern Cross, Western Australia, was built in about 1930 by a man called Lindberg. During World War II it was taken over and used as a convent for nuns. The local cricket and tennis clubs use the barbecue and shower facilities and, along with a few tourists and truckies, keep the pub going. The hairdresser shop, bakery and butcher shop have been demolished and even the railway station which operated across the road until 1960 is now located a few kilometres down the track at the wheat silos.*

to circulate and provided cooler sleeping areas. In extremely hot regions, pubs were built on stilts and roofs were pitched at high angles to reduce the trapping of heat; swing doors allowed privacy without contributing further to stifling conditions; refrigerators kept beer cold and hand pumps were used for the pouring of beer. Social functions were held in the hotels and in many isolated areas hotel rooms were still used for church services and school classes.

Left: *The hotel at Roseberry in west Tasmania, 55 kilometres north of Queenstown. Gold was discovered here in 1893 and the British Prime Minister, Lord Roseberry, lent his name to the town which quickly grew up. Regarded as a 'company town', its existence depends on the workings of the Electrolytic Zinc Company.*

The Farmer's Arms Hotel not only dominates the corner but presides over the town of Nhill, Victoria. Built from the wealth of the surrounding wheatfields, the hotel's fine verandahs are both decorative and functional.

A fine cluster of Victorian buildings harmonise in the peaceful city of York, located in the Avon Valley 100 kilometres east of Perth. Facing the ornate Town Hall (1911), the Imperial Hotel was built of stone in 1886 but lost its verandah after being extensively damaged by an earthquake in 1968.

Discovered in 1830 by Ensign Robert Dale, the rich countryside was quickly taken up and the town gazetted in 1836. When goldminers flocked to the Yilgarn diggings in 1889, York became the supply depot and the town grew until the railways were extended and the miners bypassed the district. Many tourists visit this charming town, which is surrounded by lush undulating hills on which mixed agriculture is carried out, contributing to Perth's food supplies.

A warm glow from the Macquarie Inn makes a welcome sight as a wild storm threatens. Built in 1982 by Gwen and Jim Crampton, this splendid hotel at Dubbo, New South Wales, is one of Australia's gems—in harmony with its landscape and reflective of its rural district. Its classic corrugated-iron roof dominates the surrounds while inside, the high, splendidly shaped ceilings and large open areas create a sense of spaciousness and freedom.

A wealthy farming district, Dubbo's first inn was built in 1839 by Robert Dulhunty to relieve the pressure of travellers asking for accommodation at his station homestead. The original Macquarie Inn, a long slab building with many verandah posts supporting a wonderful shingle roof, was built by Nickolas Hyeronimus in 1847 and was licensed in January 1849. As in many other prosperous and growing towns, breweries were established at Dubbo and the number of licensed hotels rapidly swelled to fifty-seven in 1900.

45

Lovely cast-iron enhances this substantial country pub at Ganmain, situated between Wagga Wagga and Narrandera, New South Wales. Rich in the wheat, sheep and cattle industries, the district's wealth is reflected in its splendid buildings, built after the railway line from Narrandera to Junee was finished in 1881.

Below: Beautifully proportioned simple buildings (among them the Keilor Hotel) form an imaginative streetscape in Keilor, an outer suburb of Melbourne.

Bottom left: The baa bar!—In the showground at Lithgow, New South Wales.

Bottom right: This attractive stone hotel (the Royal House) with its pretty roofline and narrow lace balcony, and its decorative doorways and windows, is in the seafaring town of Port Broughton, approximately 70 kilometres south of Port Pirie, South Australia.

Right: *Featuring Lex Davidson's racing car in the window, the Country Club Hotel at Longford, Tasmania, is a two-storey brick building constructed in 1850.*

The waters of the Southern Ocean at Streaky Bay, South Australia. Located on the western coast of the Eyre Peninsula and just south-east of Ceduna, is this safe all-weather port which Pieter Nuijts in the Gulden Zeepaard *examined in 1627. It was reinvestigated in 1802 by Matthew Flinders who identified it by its streaky waters. In the early 1860s storekeeper William Campbell carved a niche in the rocks and began a store around which the town grew. Streaky Bay's hotels cater for the maritime thirsts, and those of the local wheat growers and graziers.*

The Six O'Clock Swill

Throughout Australia's short history there were always those opposed to liquor and the hotel trade. These people took every opportunity to make known the evils of drink and cite examples of the harm caused by alcohol. They condemned all those connected with the operation of pubs and fought long campaigns to have hotels abolished. But it wasn't until the 1880s and 1890s that pressure from the Temperance Societies was felt in all States. Anti-liquor propaganda and pro-prohibition arguments were printed, narrated and demonstrated. In State Parliaments they demanded the reduction of hotel numbers, shorter opening hours for pubs, lower percentage alcohol and a higher drinking age.

Their campaigns were constant and intense. Sunday closing had been forced in Victoria in 1854, and was introduced in New South Wales in an Act passed in 1882. Hotel owners and large numbers of the public objected, and defied the law by secretly drinking in the 'closed' pubs. By hiring out beds for a shilling a night to 'bona fide guests', publicans used a loophole in the law to continue their Sunday trading. In South Australia, Sunday drinkers had to have walked at least 5 miles (8 kilometres) from their homes to a pub in order to buy a drink legally (prior to 1879 they had been required to travel only 1 mile [1.6 kilometres]). Closing time had been set at 11.00 p.m. for six nights of the week, and magistrates no longer had the power to issue licences. The drinking age had been raised.

Those in favour of prohibition relentlessly worked towards their goal. Renmark and Mildura were forbidden by their respective State Parliaments to allow any hotel to operate in their districts. Not all the townsfolk approved of this restrictive measure and many bought liquor smuggled from barges on the Murray River.

Polls for the prohibition of hotels occurred from State to State. The Local Option allowed for a vote to be cast for an increase or reduction of hotel numbers, and this led to many hotels being closed. Victoria even made law an Act prohibiting pensioners from receiving their pensions if they had been convicted more than twice for drunkenness during the two years prior to their pension application. New South Wales brought in a similar but less severe law.

Temperance workers moved to replace hotels with 'dry hotels', which they called Coffee Palaces. These they established in commanding positions and offered accommodation, meals and refreshments but no alcohol. They operated on a share basis and, although for a time business flourished, they all eventually closed or were taken over and run as hotels.

With World War I came cries that the pubs should close early. Temperance forces petitioned and presented thousands of signatures to Parliament. This, sparked by a drunken rampage of soldiers that caused extensive damage to properties and people in Liverpool's streets, brought to a climax the arguments in favour of earlier closing times. In 1916, a referendum, providing a choice of hourly times from 6.00 p.m. to 11.00 p.m., resulted in a majority vote for 6.00 p.m. closing of hotels—and New South Wales, South Australia, Tasmania and Victoria decided on 'temporary' reforms until the war was over. This resulted in a phenomenon which became known as the 'six o'clock swill'. Patrons, eager to get as much drinking done as possible before the pubs closed, drank frantically from knock-off time until 6.00 p.m. putting great pressure on bar staff and facilities.

In the face of stern opposition from the Temperance Societies, many publicans attempted to make their hotels more attractive and to offer better service. One such service was the free counter lunch, a gilding on the ginger-

The Lawson Park Hotel at the centre of the rich pastoral and wine-growing district of Mudgee, New South Wales, was built in the 1860s by W. Coleman and was originally known as the Tattersalls.

The area was first settled in the early 1820s and plans for the city were drawn up by Robert Hoddle. When gold was discovered in the 1860s the region received a great population influx. Writer Henry Lawson grew up in the area, going to school at the local Roman Catholic school.

Top: *The lovely Nandawar Inn with its pretty timber and iron lacework is in the northern New South Wales town of Moree. Situated on the Gwydir River between Narrabri and Goondiwindi, wheat, sheep and cattle have been produced in the fertile district since the 1850s. Edward Dickens, son of the famous Charles, was an inspector in the district and is buried in the local cemetery.*

Above: *The Sandy Creek Hotel, established in 1867 at Sandy Creek, South Australia, has a lovely roofline culminating in a bull-nose verandah supported by turned wooden posts and decorated by a series of old mirrored advertisements.*

Australian's oldest theatre was established in Hobart in 1837 and regarded by Lord Olivier as 'the best little theatre in the world' and by Dame Sybil Thorndike as the best theatre out of London. When entertainers arrived from abroad, Hobart was usually the first Australian port of call, and most performed in the plush Georgian setting of this theatre. In the bowels of the building was the 'Old Shades', a drinking place which was supposed to be haunted. Today's spirits run in the Theatre Royal Hotel next door.

bread of booze that was quickly adapted by every hotel in Australia, and which often provided an extensive and enticing range of food. Initially there was a charge for such trimmings, but competition was fierce and the fees were soon dropped. But such a utopian state of affairs could not last: in all States but Victoria and Tasmania this splendid (but expensive) service was stopped by the licensed victuallers in 1912; Victoria's free counter lunches were abolished in 1918; and it was only during World War II, as a result of food shortages, that Tasmania's pubs were forced to abandon the custom.

The passing of the free counter lunch was celebrated by the *Bulletin*, in September 1912, with the publication of 'The Dirge of the Vanished Sydney Counter Lunch':

> The corned beef torn as if by dogs,
> The slashed and riddled cheese,
> The gnawed and nibbled feet of hogs,
> Farewell! Farewell to these!
>
> Farewell to the disordered bread!
> Butter we'll see no more!
> Strew crumbs upon each mourner's head,
> Strew bones upon the floor;
>
> No longer will a pot of beer
> Suffice for every need,
> For grog has grown too blessed dear,
> Each one must BUY his feed.

… and on the dirge droned, for another thirty-two turgid lines.

The 1880s and 1890s had seen a boom in pubs, but by 1900 there was little charm to be found in newly built hotels. Gross and ugly red-brick boxes, partially 'decorated' with unimaginative bathroom tiles, sprang up all over the country. Country pubs were no longer being designed with thought for their situation or specific needs; beautiful old pubs were demolished, or their character was destroyed by re-modelling in the new taste or latest grotesque fashion.

The introduction of 6.00 p.m. closing (in most States) in 1916 completed the decline. Gone were the days of civilised social drinking when men and women could gather as much for the company and atmosphere of a pub as for the drinks it served. No entertainment was provided (as it had been in the 'good old days'), and before long most pubs had a bottle department to cater for customers who preferred drinking at home to drinking at their local hostelry—or who simply weren't permitted to stay on at their drinking hole after the magic hour of 6.00 p.m. The drinker, too, was limited in his choice of pubs. With such little drinking time available after work, men were generally forced to drink at a pub close to where they worked. These pubs had extended their bars the length of the room, or smashed out walls to make large bar rooms. Tiles for easy cleaning covered the bar face and the lower 1.8 metres of the walls, and the floor was covered in linoleum.

Immediately after the war few new hotels were built.

The impressive Empire Hotel in the mining town of Queenstown, on the rugged west coast of Tasmania, was built in 1901. Its unusual arcaded verandah gives it great individuality and stature, as does its beautiful blackwood staircase—measures of the mineral wealth surrounding the town.

Melbourne and Sydney experienced major architectural changes following a law prohibiting verandah posts to stand on footpaths. Down came the lovely verandahs and balconies and in their place drab awnings were erected. Dull-faced hotels were made less attractive by the addition of tiles on the outside walls. At some hotels these were relieved by rural or sporting paintings by Jardine, Rousel, Hanke, Baker or Woodman. Furnishings were generally cheap and alterations were made for increased speed of service rather than attractiveness.

The 1930s Depression forced many pubs to close, but from the boom period that followed new hotels emerged as ugly characterless boxes—the forerunners of today's skyscrapers. People showed their objection to sterile, un-

Covered in creeper, the Caledonian Inn, overlooking Guichen Bay at Robe, South Australia, was built in 1859 when the harbour was a very busy port, complete with customs house.

During 1856–58, following the government tax of £10 for every Chinese entering Victoria, over 16 000 Chinese landed in Robe and walked to the goldfields. The hotel became the convalescent home for the poet Adam Lindsay Gordon after he broke a few bones while breaking in a horse. He married the hotelkeeper's wife's niece, Maggie Park, who had nursed him. In 1887 the spirit of the hotel was changed when it became a parsonage. It is now used as an inn by villagers and tourists.

interesting, restrictive pubs by joining clubs that offered a congenial atmosphere, good service, cheaper prices and much longer trading hours.

During World War II, a liquor shortage made trade difficult for hotels. Pubs were forced to restrict their sales to a few hours a day and ration the number of bottles that could be bought. They staggered their opening times and many people went from pub to pub for their drinks.

In 1947 Australians were asked if they wanted 6.00 p.m. closing to remain in force. This referendum did not affect clubs, and the majority of the people voted for closing time to remain as it was, a restriction that remained in force in New South Wales until 1954 and until 1966 in Victoria.

It is doubtful that any but a few wowsers lamented the passing of the 'six o'clock swill'. There was nothing to recommend it, although it was a challenge to all concerned. Speed was the key to success. Tables and chairs were stripped from the rooms, glasses were stacked within easy reach, fast-flowing beer pumps were at hand and the extra 'rush' staff waited in dread in almost deserted saloon bars.

A few minutes after work had finished the bars were packed. Boisterous, shoving, shouting men jockeyed ten deep for a position at the bar. Barmaids worked in a frenzy. There was no time to stop and talk (not that the noise level permitted much to be heard). When a man finally wormed his way to the bar, his eyes flicking anxiously from the wall clock to the barmaid, he would repeat his call for the four or five schooners he wanted for his group. When finally the row of amber gold was put in front of him and he pocketed his change, he had the tricky task of somehow clasping all the glasses and trying to push his way through the packed mob that surged forward to take his place. By the time he got to his mates he was usually wearing the contents of the top third of the glasses. With no time to spare, and parched from anticipation, they quickly downed their glasses—and the next one to shout would join the mob. By the time the second man returned to the group with his spilt offerings, precious minutes had been lost and it was time for the third man to move off. After only a few minutes of this, the bar, floor and walls were frequently awash with slops. Grime from milling feet and dead cigarette butts was ground into the floor. The smell of such bars, and the insistent

The Broadway Hotel is like a pink fairyland castle looming amid Brisbane's traffic. Note the old streetlamp which hangs over the front door to light up the footpath.

clamour of shouting, swearing and cries for yet another round, made them unattractive places.

A barmaid's life at the height of the swill (those last desperate moments before the publican's cry of 'Time, gentlemen, time!') was hardly a life of bliss. But barmaids will be barmaids, and among them there have certainly been some of the greatest characters Australia has ever known—now nameless and unsung, but still remembered. Naturally enough, they were not admired by the wowsers and some ministers in the bad old days of the last century, when it was claimed that publicans employed attractive young barmaids, many of whom were prostitutes, as lures to entice men into the bars. The welfare of the girls, who often worked without a break for eighteen hours a day in places with no amenities for women, seemed of minor importance. In his book, *The Drink Problem in Australia*, Archdeacon Boyce expressed his opinion of barmaids in the following verses:

> Wanted, a beautiful barmaid,
>   To serve at a City bar;
> A plain-looking girl would mar trade,
>   And would prove too slow by far.
> Her eyes must be blue as a violet,
>   Or as black as a jetty sloe:
> But they must not be over modest,
>   But sparkle, and burn, and glow!
>
> Wanted, a beautiful barmaid,
>   To shine in a drinking den;
> To entrap the youth of the nation,
>   And ruin the City men;

Above: *The bar of the Family Hotel in the remote New South Wales town of Tibooburra. Artist Russell Drysdale left his mark on the pub wall in the form of a mural, as has famous artist Clifton Pugh, pictured here with aviator and businessman Dick Smith.*

To brighten destruction's pathway,
 False gleams with dark fate to blend;
To stand near Despair's dark gateway,
 To hide Sin's sad bitter end ...

In 1884, a bill to abolish barmaids in hotels was presented to the Legislative Council of New South Wales. It was defeated. The following year a similar bill was defeated in Victoria, but it became illegal to employ barmaids who were not already working in bars or who were under twenty years of age. Private bars, and those who ran them, received much criticism but they continued to operate.

In 1908 the South Australian Government passed a Licensing Bill which required working barmaids with more than three months' experience to be registered. No other women were to be employed for barwork. It wasn't until 1967 that the Government passed a bill allowing women to serve in bars.

The Victorian Government, in 1916, introduced similar legislation to that presented in South Australia eight years before. With a labour shortage in 1943 the law was relaxed and a few years later when pressure was again brought for the removal of barmaids, the threat of a liquor strike prevented their dismissal.

Most of the men who used pubs preferred barmaids to barmen. Herbert Hoover, who later became President of the United States of America, wrote romantic poetry to his sweetheart who was a barmaid at Hannan's Hotel in Kalgoorlie, Western Australia.

The attitudes of the barmaids and licensee are reflected by the attitudes of their customers. In a good pub there is a mutual respect, with 'mine host' recognising his or her responsibility to the community. One woman publican we met in an isolated area draws lonely farming families to the hotel for Saturday evening get-togethers. Armchairs arranged in front of a roaring fire in a homely room make a welcoming setting for those wanting to talk. In

At the junction of the Ovens and King Rivers in north-east Victoria, Wangaratta bears the name of pioneer settler George Faithfull's property. It was here that William Clarke established a punt to aid stock crossing the river and an inn which provided accommodation and refreshments to weary travellers and drovers.

Now a large city through which the Hume Highway passes, Wangaratta's hotels still offer accommodation and hospitality to weary travellers. The Council Club Hotel is one pub which has witnessed an evolution in mode, growth and speed of road transportation.

Below: *With its five hotels, tavern and camping area, the Yulara Tourist Village in the Northern Territory overlooks the magnificent Olgas. The village opened in 1984 and houses tourists desiring accommodation when visiting Ayers Rock and the Olgas. The land, owned by Aborigines, is leased to the National Parks and Wildlife Service.*

another room, the piano rings out as people dance and play darts. She organises dinners, sporting competitions, finds jobs for those who need them, and encourages people in their work. Like most fine 'mine hosts', she has the ability to generate warmth and good humour. She can make strangers feel welcome and provides a congenial atmosphere for the 'regulars'.

Where there is a good publican who is honest and fair, and takes pride in his or her work and hotel, there is never any trouble. If people enjoy the place in which they drink they will take care of it—and make sure other people do likewise. In one incident, at a pub in a mining area of the Northern Territory, two lads were shaping up for a fight. One fellow was a big husky leather-skinned man with fists as big as plates and a face to match. The aggressor, a skinny knobbly-kneed freckle-faced character, danced around his opponent calling on him to fight. Just as the first punch was about to be launched the publican yelled 'Stop, or neither of ya will git a drink 'ere agin!' Fists and eyes dropped and each man returned to his corner of the bar.

This lovely inn, built by George Aitchison in 1834 near the Carring-
ton Mill at Oatlands, Tasmania, is one of numerous Georgian
buildings which have been preserved in the town. It was originally
called the Lake Frederick Inn after the lake from where its stone was
quarried. In 1837 its name changed to the Lake Dulverton when the
woolgrower and transport magnate Samuel Page bought it. Its name
changed again in 1853 to the Turf then later to the White Horse.

Right above: *In the lovely fertile hills of Nimbin, 30 kilometres*
north of Lismore, New South Wales, stands the Freemason's Hotel.
Rich in agriculture, the serenity of Nimbin has attracted many city
people who have come here to develop an alternative lifestyle.

Right: *Slab walls, rough-hewn rafters, shingle roof (now covered in*
iron), simple furnishings and a sawdust-covered floor form the Old
Canberra Inn. In 1857 John Shumack built this simple cottage as his
home and took out a licence in 1876 for it to become the first public
house in the area. It was bought by John Read in 1887, named The
Pines, and remained within the family for almost 100 years before it
was reopened as a pub. It is fascinating to ponder the fact that this
humble and somewhat vulnerable timber building was in service
before the wrangle between Sydney and Melbourne over the site of
Australia's capital was settled in 1908.

The beautifully turned-out Carlton-United team rests outside the bar at the Orange Field Day, an agricultural show at Orange, New South Wales. Once a familiar sight around the city pubs, the Clydesdales and wagons loaded with old wooden beer barrels provide great interest.

Built of locally quarried bluestone, the substantial Kooringa Hotel was built to cater for the thirsty miners of Kooringa and Burra Burra in South Australia.

The discovery of copper in the district in 1845 resulted in the formation of two mining syndicates: the Princess Royal Mining Association (the 'Nobs') and the South Australian Mining Association (the 'Snobs'). As the area was unsurveyed, the law required each purchase a minimum of 20 000 acres (about 8000 hectares) at the princely sum of £1 per acre. They joined forces then divided the property, the 'Snobs' winning the site of what was to be the famous Burra Burra mine. Welsh, Cornish and German free immigrants were attracted to the district and by 1851 the population had grown to over 5000. For their employees the company built houses, churches, shops and hotels, outside which regular wrestling and boxing bouts were wagered upon.

Right above: *A gig rests over the second-storey verandah roof of Trainor's Hotel at Kilmore, Victoria.*

A rich dairying and pastoral district 60 kilometres north of Melbourne, Kilmore was first settled in 1837 by squatters migrating from New South Wales. William Routledge bought a large belt of land in 1841, naming it Kilmore after his Irish birthplace. By the 1850s the market town was thriving as it became a resting place on the daily coach run from Melbourne to the Beechworth goldfields. The railway reached the town in 1872 after which it was bypassed as the railway carried people to further destinations.

Right: *Facing each other at Echuca, Victoria, stand the Hotel American and the Palace Hotel.*

The area was once known as Hopwood's Ferry after a former convict who operated a punt and pontoon bridge at the end of which was his inn, the Criterion. At the junction of the Murray and Campaspe Rivers, and just downstream from where the Goulburn joins the Murray, the town serviced three States by river, road and rail, becoming the largest Australian inland port and second-largest Victorian port. Paddlesteamers operating on the Murray, Darling and Murrumbidgee Rivers would unload their valuable wool and timber cargoes which were then railed to Melbourne. As the railways crept across the outback the river trade fell. Many of the old pubs which experienced the hustle and bustle of the rich river trading town still stand today.

The Last Round

The aim of our pub crawl was to experience as much as possible of the whole aspect and services of pubs and those characters who have made them unique. We compared them with clubs and motels—few of which we found attractive or interesting. We were delighted at the treasures we discovered in some pubs and captivated by the beauty and magnificent situations of others. We were constantly excited by the anticipation of the next pub and amused by the splendid humour displayed in many. We were horrified by the gross additions that had been tacked onto what were already beautiful pubs and saddened when we saw lovely hotels being demolished to be replaced by cold unimaginative steel and glass boxes.

Too many of the hotels being built today are monsters compared with the pubs we have from yesteryear. We copy from abroad unimaginative, unsuitable, charmless, stereotyped skyscrapers that destroy the very spirit of this country. Overseas visitors are delighted and excited by the large variety and fascinating architecture of our old pubs, but horrified that we are ignoring their plight and the history of our country; too many priceless and irreplaceable gems have already fallen.

Many old pubs rich in beauty and splendour could be restored to capture the history and character of their era and areas. Hotels could easily and inexpensively reflect the excitement and glory of local history, or display interesting artefacts on their walls. Early farming instruments or mining tools could be hung around the bars to make them more attractive; extracts from explorers' journeys, poets' works or bushrangers' activities could make fascinating displays; artwork, plants, photographs and unusual objects could add a pleasant atmosphere to bars; verandahs and balconies, once so popular with loquacious politicians, could be utilised as attractive drinking areas with the addition of tables and chairs, a few potted palms and perhaps some colourful umbrellas.

Amid the jarrah forests, the tiny town of Pinjarra on the banks of the Murray River 85 kilometres south of Perth, Western Australia, is the hub of the dairying and timber industries of the surrounding rich countryside. People began to settle in the area in the early history of the Swan River colony and in the 1830s it was the scene of an Aboriginal massacre. When a soldier was killed by Aborigines in 1834, the 'Battle of Pinjarra' resulted—a retaliation in which fifteen Aborigines were shot.
The brick and timber Premier Hotel is large for a small town.

Right: The Jolly Miller is reminiscent of 'the pubs of old' with its swinging sign over its doorway to illustrate the house's name for those who couldn't read. The attractive ivy-clad stone public house is part of a large tourist complex which began when a substantial stone cornmill, built in 1825 at Barton, was removed and re-erected in Launceston, Tasmania. A wheelwright workshop, blacksmith shop, old water mill and museum were soon added. The tastefully appointed complex continued to grow, incorporating a motel and the Penny Royal Gun Powder Mill in the city's Cataract Gorge.

Left: The bar at the Perth Agricultural Show.

We found that Australians as a whole do not want plushness—they want drinking areas with character. There are a few hotels that have achieved this. One of the finest examples is the fascinating Dora Dora Hotel at Talmalmo, New South Wales. Alf Wright and his wife, with the help of thousands of customers, have collected numerous artefacts which are displayed on the walls, ceiling and verandah; it is such a warm friendly place, with so much interest and fine 'mine hosts', that one finds it difficult to leave.

Why not convert some of our historic relics to pubs? Along the Murray River paddlesteamers, which have served the area well, could be restored and licensed as hotels. A retired flying boat or other old aircraft could be made into a fascinating bar.

The New York Hotel at Sovereign Hill, Ballarat, is part of a museum village which is a re-creation of an old goldmining town. One can enjoy drinks in the hotel's elaborate bar while appreciating the excellent work of bygone coopers. Fine meals are served in the dining room and entertainment is provided in the theatre connected to the bar.

The situations of some old pubs are spectacular. Tucked away in breathtaking environments, cosy pubs harmonise with their surroundings and are spoilt only by ugly architectural changes or hideous power poles and lines.

Left above: Ornate plaster and the non-original balcony railing decorate the facade of the Freemason's Hotel at Toodyay, a small town 85 kilometres north-east of Perth, Western Australia. The original pub was built by W. T. Tregonning in 1861. It was bought in 1891 by H. Davey who extended the building and added a storey.

The district was first settled in the 1830s and after many floods the small township (then known as Duidgee) was moved 2 kilometres upstream. The new town was named Newcastle but changed in 1911 to Toodyay to prevent confusion with the city in New South Wales.

Left: Winton's watertower and waterhole! In the heart of the Queensland outback cattle country north-west of Longreach, sits Winton. Named by the first postmaster, Robert Allen, the town had its beginnings with a pub and store in 1875. In 1891 during the famous shearers' strike, over 500 men were camped outside of town.

Lovely wide verandahs decorated with fine lace are a splendid feature of the two-storey brick Criterion Hotel at Sale, Victoria. Built in 1865 and near the oldest standing hotel in Gippsland, its original timber verandah was partially demolished by a bolting horse pulling a butcher's cart.

Sale, named after a distinguished British army officer who fought in India and Afghanistan, was originally called Flooding Creek and later the Heart by Governor La Trobe, who referred to it as 'the heart of the Gippsland'. It grew as a camp for drovers and facilitated the Gippsland and Monaro pastoralists. When oil was struck at Omeo in 1851, Sale's importance grew, as it did in the 1860s when it supplied goods to the goldfields to its north. Today Sale is the administration centre for the Bass Strait oil and gas fields, has a large RAAF training base and a wealthy rural community.

This warm friendly looking pub at Grong Grong, New South Wales, 20 kilometres east of Narrandera in the Riverina, has a farming community as its clientele. The first part of the hotel (left) was built in the 1880s and the white corner wing was added in 1923.

They are an integral part of the community and help to make life more pleasant for everyone, including non-drinkers in the area.

In 1937, along the Adelaide to Darwin Overland Telegraph Line track, there was an inn every 80 miles (130 kilometres) or so. Drovers, roustabouts, stockmen, boresinkers and travellers frequented these simple oases and received fine hospitality. Today's mode of transport has eradicated the need for many pubs like these. Others have been closed because ridiculous laws have required costly alterations to meet standards that are inappropriate in such areas. Often there is nothing to take their place.

It is interesting to see a number of hotels side by side, or on each opposing corner, and curious to note the many country towns in which the war memorial 'stands guard over the pub'. On Anzac Day, flowers smother the impressive monument as the townsfolk solemnly pay tribute to those who died at war. When the service ends, old diggers pack the pub to reminisce, play two-up and pay their own form of respect to their dead comrades.

It is amusing to note the close proximity of many hotels and churches. Usually a town's two most impressive buildings, their spirits are different yet their congregations are often mutual. A priest once told us that a good pub can do as much for people as can a popular church. Both institutions are needed and where they have mutual respect for each other and co-exist in harmony, a well-balanced society is maintained. Salvation Army workers collect money in hotel bars, and substantial donations for the construction of some of our beautiful cathedrals have been received from people whose living was made from hotels and breweries. In early years some pubs provided the facilities for church services, school classes, art shows, theatres, cinemas, newspaper printing and postal and bank operations. In some isolated areas, pubs still provide many of these services.

Right: Two fine, large pubs, the Great Northern and the Exchange, vie for customers in the important shipping and railway town of Port Augusta at the tip of Spencer Gulf, South Australia.

An industrial town that has developed since 1854, Port Augusta is also the hub of a major transport system. Main roads radiate from the city which has a large coastal port. It is the terminus of the Trans-Australian Railway and the end of the Alice Springs line. The town contains large railway workshops and is service centre for outback properties. Named after the wife of Governor Young, Port Augusta also has many other fine pubs.

Right below: This pretty brick building with its simple barge-boards, dormer windows and beautiful doorways, delicately accentuated by curbed timbers, was built in 1840 and provided accommodation for the many people who flocked to Longford, Tasmania, for its famous race meetings. The building was intended to become the town's first railway station. After its licence was lost it become an old people's home before reverting to a private residence.

At Williamstown, overlooking Hobsons Bay and the city of Melbourne, stands the Prince of Wales Hotel. A quaint bluestone building with a pretty lace balcony held by wrought-iron brackets, the hotel was built prior to 1856 for surgeon John Wilkins who often used it for inquests.

We also found that regional peculiarities of pub architecture were not the only differences. The same size glass has various names depending on which State you're in. In New South Wales, Victoria, South Australia and Western Australia a 140-millilitre glass is a 'pony' but in Queensland it's a 'small beer'. In New South Wales and the Northern Territory a 200-millilitre glass is a 'seven' and in Victoria and Western Australia it's a 'glass', but in South Australia it's a 'butcher'. A 285-millilitre glass in New South Wales and Western Australia is a 'middy', in Victoria, Queensland and Tasmania it's a 'pot', in the Northern Territory a 'handle' and in South Australia a 'schooner'. A 425-millilitre glass in New South Wales, Victoria and Western Australia is a 'schooner' while in South Australia it's a 'pint'. In New South Wales a 'pint' is 575 millilitres while the same measure in Western Australia is called a 'pot'!

Because of their shape, some glasses are referred to as 'lady's waists'; 'nobbles' are small drinks of spirits or beer; and so it goes. But whatever the name of a glass, or the amount it will hold, that glass must never be whipped away by bar staff if so much as a drop remains within it!

Bottles and kegs also come in interesting shapes and sizes. The variety of bottles, their colour and labels, make an interesting display; and when empty, they are often found decorating graves, made into fences and even buildings. Legend tells that with the wind whining in the bottles near the pub at Innamincka, Burke's ghost can be heard.

Empty cans bound together to form yachts, motorboats, dinghies and canoes, which all compete in the Beer Can Regatta on the Arafura Sea, have provided means for great entertainment and an excuse for much beer drinking at Darwin. The following old verse is still appropriate to many Australians:

Beer, O Beer, I love thee;
In thee I place my trust:
I'd rather go to bed with hunger
Than go to bed with thust.

As Australians, we are wealthy in the knowledge of our past and foolish in our lack of appreciation of what the past has given us. The old pubs are perhaps some of the finest monuments in Australia, yet by our own lack of foresight and blasé attitudes we are allowing them to be demolished or ruined. By showing a few of these unique and exciting buildings, we hope that more Australians will become aware of the valuable and beautiful hotels we have and continue to make them charming places for people to gather.

A new structure in Alice Springs is the Old Alice Inn. Most of the town's early pubs have been replaced by more elaborate hotels which cater for the local population and the large tourist trade who visit the Centre.

Alice Springs was named after the wife of Charles Todd, the Superintendent of Telegraphs. It was previously known as Stuart in honour of the explorer who ventured through in 1862.

Guests of Hadley's Orient Hotel, Hobart, enjoy breakfast in the lovely Cafe Orient. Now similar to the Tiffany Room in Raffles Hotel, Singapore, the cafe before 1987 was an open courtyard garden.

A handsome stone building, the hotel was constructed in 1848 with some convict labour for John Webb, a pardoned convict. Non-commissioned military men were not allowed in the hotel which had a fine billiards room and large ballroom. It was bought in 1861 by John Hadley whose family continued operating it after his death. Roald Amundsen, first man to reach the South Pole, stayed at the hotel on his return in 1912.

Over 200 Friends of Newnes Hotel pose for a photograph having nearly completed moving and rebuilding the old pub. Located 200 kilometres west of Sydney in the spectacular Wolgan Valley, the Newnes Hotel was originally built in 1907 by John Alexander Stammers-Jones to serve the needs of workers in the old shale-oil-mining town.

After the works closed in the 1930s, most of the buildings and other structures were dismantled, leaving the picturesque pub which became popular with campers, bushwalkers, bikies, rock climbers and tourists. In August 1986 the Capertee River flooded and changed course, undermining the hotel's foundations and tearing off the storerooms, kitchens and back verandah. People from all walks of life met, formed Friends of Newnes Hotel and planned a three-weekend removal and rebuilding scheme.

A site on higher ground was chosen, cleared, foundations built and new floor constructed. All equipment, building materials, food and labour were donated. On 24, 25 and 26 July 1987, men, women, and children worked, removing the roof, dismantling walls and carrying them to their new site where they were re-erected. When complete, the old piano was carted up and a human chain was formed to move the precious amber fluid. Then celebrations began!

The Norseman Hotel, the largest building in the old Western Australian goldmining town, is a welcome sight after the long drive west across the Nullarbor. Wide streets in the rambling town are bordered by shady verandahs, essential in the hot dusty climate.

Two hundred kilometres south of Kalgoorlie, among the grey-green scrub and trees at the southern end of Lake Cowan, and framed by huge mullock heaps, Norseman was named in 1892 by prospector Laurie Sinclair after his horse. It became the main centre for the prosperous Dundas goldfields which also yielded iron, copper, manganese, gypsum, feldspar and nickel. The town site was gazetted in 1895 and the Criterion, the Freemason's and Norseman Hotels were erected. The railway was extended from Coolgardie in 1909 and there was much pressure for it to be connected to Esperance. When business was slow in the pubs, a 'Railway Indignation' rally would be held and miners would stop work for a meeting then adjourn to the pubs to fire their spirits. During the Depression of the 1930s, the town's population soared. Today reef gold is still mined and all road travellers from the eastern States pass through Norseman.

The Heritage Tavern, originally known as the Commercial Hotel, dominates the fascinating commercial streetscape of the port of Rockhampton, Queensland.

The Golden Fleece Hotel was built in 1859 on land granted by Sir George Bowen to the first town-born white child, William James Jnr. It was replaced by the sumptuous three-storey Commercial, designed by John W. Wilson and built by Mrs Leah Johnson in 1898. As its name suggests, sample rooms for travelling salesmen lured trade, and its first-class accommodation and facilities attracted country people and important visitors, including Prime Minister Mr Ben Chifley and international sporting teams. The beautiful iron lace verandahs (cast locally by the Burns and Twigg foundry) overlook the Fitzroy River, which was once a highway for the rural activities of central Queensland. Rockhampton was also a seaport for despatching gold from the Canoona and Mount Morgan fields.

Left: Burnie Inn, a single-storey, slate-roofed inn, with a simple verandah decorated by a timber valance board, was licensed in 1847 and moved in 1973 from its original site in Marine Terrace, Burnie, to its present parkland home. This quaint inn ceased to operate as a public house in 1900 but is still being visited by the many tourists who come to this industrial port on Tasmania's north-west coast.

Right: Very few of these wonderful posters, painted by artists such as Rousel, Jardine, Hanke, Baker and Woodman, still decorate the outer walls of hotels. Highly valued by collectors, most now have been placed in museums.

The Gooloogong Hotel at Gooloogong between Forbes and Cowra, New South Wales, stands opposite one of the few large log community halls remaining in Australia.

The Wilmington Hotel has a balcony but no verandah posts. The large solid pub at Wilmington, 45 kilometres east of Port Augusta, South Australia, serves the local farmers and railway workers.

The 'busy' facade of the Prince Albert Hotel at Launceston is very different to the original structure built in 1855, which was named the Terminus Hotel. The billiard hall was then a feature of the pub. Now a private hotel, it reflects a Victorian prosperity and is one of only a few of the fine old pubs still standing in Tasmania's second-largest city.

The pretty Tasmanian town of Evandale, with its wonderful collection of early buildings unspoilt by modern additions, was named after Surveyor-General G. W. Evans in 1836, the same year the two-storey Prince of Wales was built. Like Longford, a town nearby, the district was founded in 1808 by settlers from Norfolk Island.

Left: *The Palm Court of Sydney's Intercontinental Hotel was once part of the beautiful sandstone Treasury Building and Premier's Office. This was built in 1849 to designs drawn by Mortimer Lewis with substantial additions made in 1896 by architect Walter Vernon. When overseas investors wished to develop a multistorey hotel on the site, a condition was they could not tear down the historic building, hence it has been incorporated into the modern glass and cement tower.*

The bar at the annual race meeting on the huge Northern Territory cattle station, Brunette Downs, is a popular place.

The Terminus Hotel hides behind a more recent facade in front of Marulan's memorial. Explorer and pioneer Hamilton Hume died in this small town at the crossing of the railway line and the Hume Highway, 30 kilometres east of Goulburn, New South Wales.

Left above: *Two fine big Queensland hotels, the Tattersalls and the Barcoo, vie for custom and dominate the small town of Blackall, 200 kilometres south-east of Longreach.*

It was on a nearby station, Alice Downs, in 1892, that the famous Jack Howe, using blades, sheared 321 sheep in 7 hours 20 minutes, a record that stood until 1950 when broken by a machine shearer. The large object in the foreground on the median strip is a huge chunk of petrified wood.

Left: *A two-storey tower trimmed with lace balances like a tier on a wedding cake. The Hotel Federal at Port Pirie on Spencer Gulf, caters for the thirst of an industrial city. In the 1880s the South Australian Government built a narrow-gauge railway line from Port Pirie to Cockburn on the South Australian–New South Wales border. It was eventually linked to Broken Hill by private line and carried the great wealth of ore to the Port Pirie smelters, built by Broken Hill Proprietary Co. Ltd in 1889. The port facilities were extended greatly so large ships could take the refined loads to overseas markets.*

Above: *The small but ornate Family Hotel at the industrial city of Port Pirie, South Australia, was built in 1904.*

Governor Robe named the town in 1845 after the first vessel, John Pirie, to explore the creek on which the town sits. It was this schooner that was used to bring settlers from the United Kingdom to South Australia. The inlet was dredged and a substantial port was established when the State's northern regions began producing wheat in export quantities. After this petered out the town languished until 1889 when the Broken Hill Proprietary Co. Ltd built large smelters there and railed their ore from Broken Hill to Port Pirie for processing and shipping.

Once known as the 'Queen of the Murchison', Cue, 80 kilometres
north of Mount Magnet, Western Australia, was a thriving mining
town whose goldmines produced over 28 million grams. Named in
1892 after prospector Tom Cue, the town became the destination for
thousands of diggers. The Cue Hotel was first listed in the Western
Australian Post Office Directory in 1895–96 with Frederick Carlisle
as proprietor. The hotel closed in December 1971, adding to the
eeriness of a near-deserted, but fascinating, historic town.

Curving with the road, the impressive Shamrock Hotel, with its
decorative plaster modelling, opened in 1866. It operated as the
Farmer's Home until 1891, when it was bought by Joseph O'Hara
who changed its name to the Shamrock. Its verandah and balcony,
onto which the rooms once opened, have been replaced by an
awning. Northam, 93 kilometres east of Perth in the Avon Valley,
supports a series of very distinctive hotels.

80

*The Norman Hotel at South Brisbane was built in 1889. Fine pro-
portions incorporate a very wide verandah trimmed with iron, and a
narrow lace balcony recessed over a rounded verandah roof.*

*In the industrial city of Burnie in Tasmania sits the substantial
Cecil Hotel. Typical of many southern hotels, it has no verandah or
balcony.*

*In 1826, 50 000 acres (about 20 000 hectares) of land were taken
up at Emu Bay (Burnie) by the Van Diemen's Land Company.
When tin at nearby Mount Bischoff was found in the early 1870s, it
was transported by horse-drawn vehicles to the town, from whose
wharves it was shipped abroad.*

Large crowds in Broken Hill, New South Wales, assemble in front of the Astra Hotel during the town's Centenary celebrations.

Beside the Landsborough Highway and the railway line is the
isolated Wellshot Hotel at Ilfracombe, just east of Longreach,
Queensland. Servicing local cattle and sheep stations, the pub also
provides a welcome break for travellers on a hot day.

Right above: At Longreach, 700 kilometres west of Rockhampton,
Queensland, is the sprawling Midlander Hotel.
   Beef and sheep industries are the lifeline of this large inland town
which is noted also for the Qantas (Queensland and Northern Territory Aerial Services Ltd) hangar, which was erected in 1921 by
aviation pioneers W. Hudson Fysh and P. J. McGinness. It remained
the Qantas headquarters until 1934 and was an aircraft factory from
1926 until 1930.

Right: Warm honey-coloured sandstone with white contrasts and an
unusual roofline in brilliant red, makes the Commercial Hotel at
Cowell, South Australia, one of the country's distinctive hotels.
It is a most interesting hotel full of architectural curiosities. Some
110 kilometres south-west of Whyalla on the Eyre Peninsula, it
stands in front of the 'black stump'.

Top: *The pretty pink pub with peak-hat squat tower is the Commonwealth Hotel at Roma in south-east Queensland.*

Like the beginning of many towns, Roma grew from a station store which provided goods to travellers and nearby settlers. Stephen Spencer established Mt Abundance cattle station in 1857 and ten years later, the site gazetted, it was named after Diamantina Roma, the wife of Sir George Bowen, first Governor of Queensland. It was here also, at Romaville Winery in 1863, that S. S. Bassett produced the first commercial wine in Queensland.

Above: *Hunters Hotel was built in 1898 at Queenstown, a fascinating town amid the rugged mountains of Tasmania's west coast. Gold was first discovered in the vicinity in 1856 and people flocked to the inhos-pitable country. But it was the extraction of copper and the establishment of Mt Lyell Co. that resulted in the growth of the town and the licensing of fourteen hotels. The prosperity of the town and its five remaining pubs is totally dependent on continuing profitability of the mineral production.*

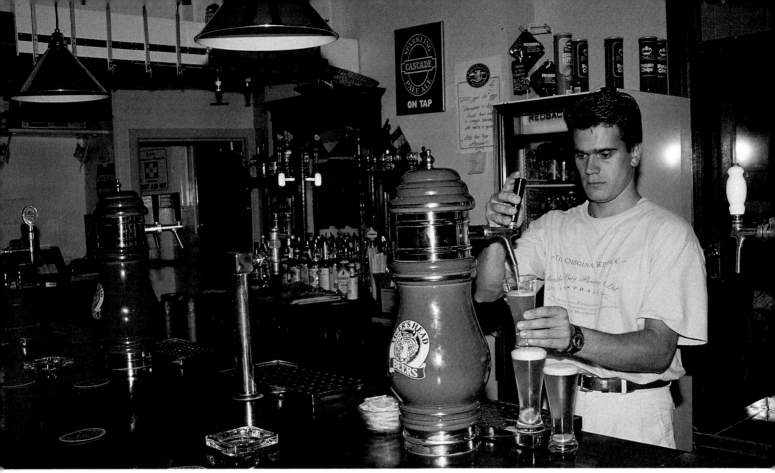

Top: *In the Brewer's Bar at the St Ives Hotel, Hobart, a beer brewed on the premises is poured. Hops were introduced to the district in 1822 and, as beer was a popular drink, breweries were established and flourished in every town. Cascade Brewery, established nearby in 1824 and now one of Australia's oldest public companies, is competing with 'boutique' beers brewed in small quantities in many traditional pubs.*

Above: *The Star, a big corner pub, is a feature of Rutherglen, which was named after the Scottish birthplace of John Wallace, who was prominent in the busy goldmining rush of the 1850s. On the southern side of the Murray River about 40 kilometres west of Albury, Victoria, Rutherglen is a wealthy wheat, wool, dairying and wine-growing district.*

The large brick Wagin Hotel, with its simple timber verandah, dominates the agricultural centre of Wagin ('Place of Emus'), 280 kilometres south-east of Perth, Western Australia.

The Avon Bridge Hotel, Northam, Western Australia. The temperance movement had a marked effect on the profitability of Northam hotels. By 1882, the Avon Bridge, which had been erected in 1858, was in a poor state of repair, so H. Leeder closed it for renovation and reopened it twelve months later. It was bought by Charles Taylor who, assured of the railway being built through the town, changed the name to the Railway Hotel. It reverted to its original name when purchased by Elliot Lockyer. Additions of red brick trimmed with stucco, and decorated with stained-glass windows, were added in 1897.

The simple stone Broken Hill Hotel at Boulder, a few kilometres from Kalgoorlie, Western Australia, was one of thirty-four pubs in the town in 1905.

Named after the famous Great Boulder mine claimed by Samuel Pearse and W. G. Brookman in 1893, Boulder became a boom town. The influx of people to Boulder led to the discovery of Kalgoorlie's Golden Mile. Mines operated twenty-four hours a day and, until the pipeline reached Kalgoorlie in 1903, water was expensive and scarce and diseases such as typhoid common. With the great wealth came the brilliant buildings, most of which still stand in both Boulder and Kalgoorlie. A poem, 'The Boulder Block' by 'Crosscut' Wilson, describes the town:

Rather rowdy,
Dingy, cloudy,
Dusty, dirty, dim and dowdy,
Thirsty throats to mock.
Can't mistake her,
Good drought slaker,
Six pubs to the bloomin' acre,
That's the Boulder Block.

Top: *On stubby piers in the sheep, wheat and cattle belt, between Mitchell and St George in Queensland's mid-south, stands the pretty Club Hotel.*

Above: *In Tasmania, amid farmlands of the South Esk River 25 kilometres south of Launceston, sits Longford, with its brilliant Victorian and Regency streetscape. Originally called Norfolk Plains after families from Norfolk Island were granted land following the failure of their settlement in 1807, the town was established in 1827. The Queen's Arms Hotel was built in 1835 by William Dadery Jnr.*

Right above: *Queensland bush humour! Two women rest on unusual seats outside the dunny of the Club Hotel between Mitchell and St George.*

Right: *Dwarfed by the skyscrapers of the beach resort Coolangatta, the Port O' Call exudes a traditional Queensland character.*
   Unfortunately many of the quaint pubs that once graced this area have been replaced by glass jungles filled with canned music and dazzling lights. Coolangatta was named by cedar cutters after Alexander Berry's Coolangatta was destroyed on nearby rocks in 1846.

Lashings of cast iron and latticework accentuate the lovely wide verandahs of Brisbane's Regatta Hotel. A three-storey rendered brick building erected by George Gazzard, it overlooks the Brisbane River and is one of the city's many fine old pubs.

North of Haddon Corner in Queensland's channel country, rests one of Australia's most isolated hotels—once a 'pub with no beer'—the Betoota. As its parched surrounds flourish briefly with life, colour and vigour after rain, so too does the pub as tourists make their way to and from the annual meeting of the Birdsville Races.

A drovers' pub, built in 1874 by Roly Nutt, and licensed to John and Mary Nutt, the Yatina Hotel took six years to construct as the stone had to be cut by hand and carted by Matthew O'Reilley's bullock team.

The town of Yatina, located on the northern side of the Goyder Line near Peterborough, was once planned to be the second-largest town in South Australia but low annual rainfalls and crop failures caused people to abandon the district. A dozen folk now reside here, but during the Bicentennial celebrations a day of festivities resulted in the consumption of fifteen 18-gallon kegs of beer (about 1300 litres), sixty-six dozen stubbies and a mountain of food. The isolated hotel is mainly a watering hole for farmers and travellers needing a break.

In front of the Post Office Hotel, Bourke, vehicles are made ready for the start of the 'Bash' which raises funds for the Variety Club charity.

Bourke was once a thriving river town to which north-western New South Wales woolgrowers sent their bales for transportation down the Culgoa and Darling Rivers to markets. To cater for the influx of thirsty bullock drivers, teamsters and workers who helped load wool onto barges, many unlicensed shanties mushroomed, some with the aid of local graziers who tired of being hospitable to large numbers of visitors. The river trade deteriorated as silting and droughts made transportation unreliable. The railway, which reached Bourke in 1885, took the trade.

The Post Office Hotel, often referred to as Fitz's, was built in 1888 by Ned Luscombe and taken over in 1891 by Paddy Fitzgerald. It still plays an important role as meeting place for locals and tourists.

The Old Grapevine Hotel flanked by the Star Theatre and Billiards Hall was built in 1866 replacing the original Star Hotel. The theatre provided a venue for plays, dances, vaudeville and community gatherings during the gold rush era at Chiltern, Victoria. In the hotel courtyard is a grapevine, reputed to be one of the oldest in the country—planted 1867 and still going strong.

An old mirror depicting Bertie the Cellarman, which is reported to be the property of Ballarat Brewing Company, graces the wall of the Canberra Hotel in Ballarat, Victoria. In 1871 the census revealed Ballarat to have 13 breweries and 477 hotels for a population nearing 47 000.

In the hot, arid former goldmining town of Leonora, Western Australia, the Central Hotel is open for business.

Explorer John Forrest, on his search in 1869 for missing Ludwig Leichhardt, named the area Mount Lenora after his niece. Gold was discovered here in the 1890s, however its twin town Gwalia outstripped it in growth. When the remarkable Sons of Gwalia mine closed in 1963, the township of Gwalia died while that of nearby Leonora continued to supply the needs of pastoral holdings. Since 1900, the streetscape of Leonora has changed little.

Below left: Eyecatching and clever advertising identifies the Shaft Tavern at New Lambton, a suburb of Newcastle, New South Wales. Coal and Newcastle are synonymous, as are miners, wharfies and steelworkers with the Shaft Tavern.

Below: The Georgetown Hotel and the general store reflect pride and good taste in the tiny South Australian hamlet of Georgetown, 50 kilometres south-east of Port Pirie.

Above: *With doorway and window surrounds accented in white, the lovely bluestone Corio Hotel at Goolwa, South Australia, was built in 1857 and opened the following year. On the lounge ceiling is a 3.6 x 7.3 metres print of a painting entitled* Spirit of '76 *by Archibald M. Willard. It is described as the most patriotic painting in America and this is the only print in Australia. The pub has its own ghost. An old black lady appears once or twice a year but causes no trouble. On the banks of Lake Alexandrina, the Corio is a popular watering hole for anglers and duck shooters.*

On Highway 1, at the small neat town of Gin Gin, 50 kilometres west of Bundaberg, Queensland, stands the Highway Hotel.

Below: *The attractive Warracknabeal Hotel in Warracknabeal, Victoria, built in 1890 features a fine Art Nouveau leadlight around its entrance. It is one of the few buildings in the town which has retained its character by keeping its decorative cast-iron verandah and balcony.*

The interesting architecture of the Victoria Inn at Williamstown draws attention. An early Melbourne suburb and port overlooking the city, Williamstown has a wonderful array of fascinating pubs and cottages.

Above left: The Cecil Hotel, Casino, New South Wales, was originally known as the Imperial before being dragged by horse and bullock teams to its present location in 1916. It became affectionately nicknamed 'the Vatican' when owner Tom Mulcahy's son Frank became a priest. The hotel serves the local farming community, the town's business interests and tourists.

In the hot centre of the Queensland cattle country between Charleville and Blackall is Tambo and its spacious Carrangarra Hotel.

Under the searing sun in the heart of Queensland is Barcaldine, a town made famous during the shearers' strike. Wide rambling verandahs of the Shakespeare, Artesian and Railway Hotels provide cool and shade and an interesting streetscape. The first Shakspeare Hotel was named after its owner George Page Shakspeare who transported his two-storey, corrugated-iron and bush-timber pub from Pine Hill to Barcaldine by bullock team in 1886. Its spelling was changed to Shakespeare when bought by Walter Crust in 1911. It was demolished in 1914 and rebuilt with 75 metres of verandah. This was burnt in 1924 and the present brick and concrete hotel opened in December 1925. The hotel's clientele are mainly shearers, railway workers, jackaroos, graziers, main road workers and a few tourists.

Above right: *St George killing the dragon is a feature of the interesting old Esk Brewery which was built in Launceston, Tasmania, in 1881.*

Right: *A couple of participants of the Great Camel Race enjoy a few drinks with the locals at the Shakespeare Hotel in Barcaldine, Queensland.*

Left: *The Booyoolee Hotel at Gladstone, South Australia, 40 kilometres east of Port Pirie, is a mixture of colour, pattern and architecture. Named in 1871 for the British Prime Minister, Gladstone sits among the wheat- and sheep-growing areas at the junction of the Broken Hill–Port Pirie and the Adelaide–Wilmington railway lines.*

Left: *Clinging to the curve of the road, with a backdrop of the bare hills of Gulf St Vincent, is the Horse Shoe Hotel at Noarlunga. About 40 kilometres south of Adelaide at the mouth of the Onkaparinga River, the old inn, reputed to have been a haven for sailors, smugglers and 'bad men', was built in the 1840s and is now a restaurant.*

Below left: *The Park Hotel in Albany, Western Australia.*
   In 1627 Dutch explorer Peter Nuyts charted the western coast. On Christmas Day 1826 troops under Major Edmund Lockyer arrived from New South Wales to take possession of the west of the continent. Lockyer named the site beside Princes Royal Harbour Frederickstown after the Duke of York and Albany, however, the town came to be known as Albany. At first the settlement was governed from New South Wales but control passed to the Swan River colony in 1831.
   With such a fine natural harbour, overseas ships visited. The mail steamers used to drop shipments and take on coal and the whaling station brought much business to Albany. The harbour was Western Australia's major port until 1900 when Fremantle Harbour was developed. Many seafaring shanties sprang up to cater for the thirsts of sailors and many large hotels bear testimony to the prosperity of the city that is cooled by the breezes off the Southern Ocean.

Some 135 kilometres west of Brisbane, in the rich farming and wheat-growing area of the Darling Downs, Toowoomba houses many fine old buildings which are a legacy of the local architectural firm Jas. Marks & Sons. The ornate White Horse was designed by James Marks and built in 1900. Its verandah, which enhanced the original building, has since been replaced by an ugly awning.
   Originally known as The Swamp, Toowoomba took its name from a property owned by Thomas Alford on what was once the wagon route between the western stations and Brisbane. Today, with its spacious gardens and magnificent trees, Toowoomba is the second-largest city in Queensland and the White Horse is one of its many fine pubs.

In the heart of the quaint Victorian goldmining town of Maldon, north of Ballarat, stands the Maldon Hotel.

Maldon was originally named Tarrangower after the mountain under which it rests, and gold was first discovered here at the end of 1853 by John Mechosk. The rush began and by 1854 approximately 20 000 miners, many of them Chinese, had flocked to the fields. Two years later, mining of the reef began, its profits making the fields the second-richest in Victoria. Today Maldon soaks up the sun, a relatively unspoilt town mirroring a fascinating mining era.

Below right: Two hundred kilometres west of Cairns, Queensland, sits Chillagoe and its pub.

Grazier W. Atherton of Chillagoe Station found copper and silver on his property in 1888. Mining began and copper, tin and silver-lead were extracted by a series of small smelters at various locations. When it became apparent that the ore needed special treatment, the Chillagoe Railway and Mines Company Ltd was formed and in 1897 began building the rail from Mareeba to Chillagoe then on to Mungana. A railway was also constructed from Almaden to Etheridge, then to Chillagoe. The large smelters, of which chimney ruins remain, were built in Chillagoe in 1901. After World War I, the liquidated company was taken over by the State Government and the smelters were reopened. They were operated until they became uneconomical in 1943. The surrounding limestone country produces wonderful formations and brilliant caves.

On the lonely dirt road in the remote New South Wales outback between Balranald and Ivanhoe, is an oasis, the Homebush Hotel built in 1878. A social centre for station people, the cool beer garden provides a convivial atmosphere for tall yarns, a few jokes and plenty of chat.

Above: *On the South Australian border 60 kilometres west of Broken Hill, sits the tiny town of Cockburn. When Broken Hill was producing so much valuable silver-lead in the 1880s, the South Australian Government built a narrow-gauge railway line from Port Pirie (at which Broken Hill Associated Smelters were duly built) to the border at Cockburn. The New South Wales Government refused to extend the rail but in 1886 passed an Act permitting the Silverton Tramway Company to build and run a narrow gauge rail to link Broken Hill with Cockburn.*

The Railway Hotel serves people from the surrounding district.

Below: *Some 25 kilometres to the east of Hobart in rich undulating country sits Richmond, a lovely old village which boasts Australia's oldest surviving bridge and Roman Catholic church. Explored in 1803 by John Bowen, land was granted to free settlers, military officers and government men and the town was proclaimed by Governor Sorell on 23 February 1824. An important convict centre and military establishment, it became a valuable wheat-producing area and by the 1830s was Tasmania's third-largest town.*

The impressive Richmond Arms was built of local stone in 1888, two years after fire destroyed the Lennox Arms which graced the site from 1827. A stone stable remains. Today, the lovely village, with its beautiful Victorian and Georgian buildings, is a major drawcard for tourists.

Top: *A great name for a pub, the Wobbly Boot, at Boggabilla, New South Wales.*

A sleepy little town south of the Macintyre River near Goondiwindi, Boggabilla is the centre of a sheep and cattle industry.

Above: *The very attractive Lakes Creek Hotel is another of the splendid early buildings at Rockhampton, Queensland.*

The area was explored in 1853 by Charles and William Archer, who named the Fitzroy River and took up land they called Gracemere. In 1856 the Commissioner of Crown Lands chose a site for a town but two years later only a store and an inn had been built. In 1858 when gold was discovered on the neighbouring property of

Canoona, people flocked by ship to the port of Rockhampton and although the gold rapidly petered out, many folk stayed and established properties and businesses. A regular steamer service to Brisbane began in 1860 and as pastoral properties grew, Rockhampton became the central port for imports and exports, which were boosted considerably by the discovery of the great goldmine at nearby Mount Morgan.

The wealth from the area is reflected in the brilliant array of buildings erected, the beautiful gardens and the massive shade trees. By 1900, the problem of river silting became apparent and the connection of the railway to Brisbane meant most goods were transported by rail, hence the port lost its importance.

109

Hundreds of people enjoyed themselves and danced the 'Chicken' in the Hofbrauhaus at Brisbane's World Expo '88.

This colourful character portrays the relaxed carefree image of the
Aussie drinker. Cartoonist Ken Maynard's Ettamogah Pub and its
characters have come to life since Lindsay and Sonia Cooper opened
the Ettamogah Hotel near Albury, New South Wales.

A substantial stone pub serves the needs of a sparsely populated arid
area of the southern end of the Birdsville Track, South Australia.
    Marree, whose name means 'Place of Possums', became a depot
for the Afghan camel drivers. It was named Hergott after an artist
on John McDouall Stuart's 1859 expedition but was proclaimed the
town Marree in 1883.

This very attractive stone hotel, with its beautiful verandah and balcony, is the Shirley at the small town of Bethungra, 24 kilometres south-west of Cootamundra on the Olympic Highway, New South Wales.

The old dray and waterpump add character to the pretty Carritor Hotel in the northern region of the spectacular Flinders Ranges in South Australia. Hawker, 100 kilometres north-east of Port Augusta, proved to be heartbreak country for many of the families who toiled the land for years, only to see the drought swallow their stock and crops.

Below: *The substantial Bordertown Hotel at Bordertown near the South Australian–Victorian border was first licensed in 1869 and was relocated three blocks away in 1903. Built by James Simpson, the pub is full of characters from many walks of life: farmers, meat workers, truckies, stock agents, shearers and businessmen. Locals tell the story of Harry Dwyer, a 75-year-old horse trainer, who with a mate, both dressed as Indians, rode through the bar and up the stairs. An old fellow at the bar was so alarmed he fell off his stool.*

Then there is Les Wilkinson who at ninety-five still slowly rides his bike but halts quickly to lift his cycle over shadows cast by telegraph poles. And Bertie Dyer, who boasts he is the only 'legalised one arm bandit in town'—in a fire he lost half of his right hand, his left arm and part of his foot. Another colourful character is Dick Hartman, who is always bringing up the issue of land rights and claims the hotel as a sacred site. Bordertown is renowned for its annual national camel races held each November.

Bottom: *This neat stone hotel on the Eyre Highway at Wudinna, South Australia, between Port Augusta and Ceduna, caters for the local grazing industry and traffic heading across the Nullarbor.*

Perched on the open plains beside Highway 31, just north of Albury, New South Wales, is the Ettamogah Pub. Cartoonist Ken Maynard, who was born at Albury, established the pub in his comic strip in Australasian Post over twenty years ago. The fun and humour it generated inspired Lindsay 'Coop' Cooper and his wife Sonia to build the pub. With its old Chevrolet utility (deposited in a flood), the dog Bandit outside his kennel, barmen dressed in their best stubbies, boots and black singlets, the pub opened in 1987 and is constantly flocked by tourists.

The merits of the beer at the Ettamogah Pub are modestly spelt out on the side of the building.

Top: *Shindy's Inn, a small simple pub at Louth beside the Darling River, New South Wales. The original Louth Hotel was operating in 1865 and housed the community's post office. Today, the tiny town is a meeting place for woolgrowers and their employees, and hosts thousands of locals and visitors at the annual picnic races.*

Above: *Two large hotels dominate the small rural town of Junee, New South Wales, which was once called Loftus.*

When it was announced that the railway would pass through the town, Thomas Edmonds bought a block of land opposite where he hoped the station would be erected. With only one licence available for the district, it was a race to get the Loftus built before the completion of the Royal which had already been started. In six weeks William Chalmers had the Loftus standing and in 1884 it received the licence.

The Royal remained without a permit for some years until one was purchased from the Conqueror Hotel. Additions were made in 1896 and 1909 making it one of Australia's leading hotels outside the metropolitan areas. A porter met all trains and the verandahs were used as a banquet hall on special occasions. Being halfway between Sydney and Melbourne, Junee was a popular place for commercial travellers and businessmen who needed rest for the night. To cash in on such market, the Commercial was built in 1915.

Right: *A pub with many brands of beer. The Halfway Hotel near Horrocks Pass is located between Wilmington and Port Augusta, South Australia.*

Above: *An open octagonal tower dominates the two-storey Grand Hotel built in 1901 on a hill overlooking the old mining town of Mount Morgan, 40 kilometres south-west of Rockhampton, Queensland.*

Gold was discovered here in 1882 by Thomas and Edwin Morgan who formed a company and began one of the most productive goldmines in the State. In the early 1900s copper was found under the gold deposits and a fortune was taken from the earth. In 1927, when extraction had become more difficult, costs had risen and prices had dropped, the Mount Morgan Gold Mining Company went into liquidation. Two years later it was bought by Mount Morgan Ltd and open-cut mining continues to extract wealth from the ground. What was once a distinguished mountain is now a giant hole in the ground.

A cobra, as distant from its Indian homeland as the William Creek Hotel is from civilisation. In the desolate heart of South Australia to the west of Lake Eyre, where remnants of forgotten dreams form piles of rubble in the remote shifting sands, is William Creek.

With opulent roofline combining a number of architectural styles, Adelaide's Stag Hotel is one of the city's most unusual pubs.

Stoppys Waterfront Inn at Salamanca Place, Hobart, is part of the finest array of Georgian waterfront warehouses in Australia.

In the 1830s a new wharf on the southern side of Sullivans Cove was being built using convict labour housed in a hulk moored alongside. From 1835 to 1860, merchants and shipowners in the great seafaring and whaling port built the three- and four-storey warehouses and chandleries. Ships from the other side of the world moored in front while goods were unloaded and wool and minerals despatched. To cater for the needs of men working in the stores and thirsty sailors, inns, generally with salty names such as the Whaler's Return, the Neptune Inn and the Shipwright's Arms, sprang amid the warehouses. Today most of these important buildings house crafts, arts and souvenir businesses, with numerous restaurants and tourists attractions.

A very pretty Court House Hotel is a welcoming sight to those entering Nathalia, Victoria. Situated south of the Murray River between Echuca and Tocumwal, the small town rests amid magnificent stands of giant red gums many of which speak of a past era of Aboriginal life, their carvings and canoe scars a memorial to the lost Bangarang tribe.

Top: *An interesting series of buildings in the main street of the Tasmanian west coast mining town of Zeehan. Named by Bass and Flinders after one of the ships of Abel Tasman, who sighted the peak of Mt Zeehan in 1642, Zeehan was a small silver-lead mining town by 1882. Ore in quantity and quality was found over such a wide area that by 1901 the population was over 5000, making it the third-largest Tasmanian town. By 1909 when the town boasted twenty-six pubs, the mines began to fail. The recent reopening of the Renisson Bell Tin Mine and the proximity to Queenstown, 38 kilometres to the south, has left the town alive, the Central Hotel being one of the town's two surviving pubs.*

Above: *The lovely dining room of the Georgian St Andrew's Inn at Cleveland, Tasmania.*

Right: *Built in 1845 with convict labour, the St Andrew's Inn at Cleveland, is one of the many coaching inns now open for tourists.*

Right above: *South of Gladstone in Queensland near Seventeen Seventy, a Captain Cook landmark, is Miriam Vale, a sleepy little village bypassed by the Bruce Highway and unspoiled by developers. The impressive timber pub, framed by huge old trees, dominates the town.*

Above: *The Grand Hotel at Healesville, a popular resort at the junction of Grace Burn and the Watts River, a short distance north-east of Melbourne.*

Surrounded by five mountain peaks of the Great Dividing Range, the district is famous for its spectacular scenery, its wildlife and magnificent forests.

Left: *Large crowds assemble at Broken Hill, New South Wales, outside the Astra Hotel during the town's Centenary celebrations.*

Right top: *The rather grand brick Quairading Hotel, with its fine verandah and attractive balcony, stands in the small rural settlement of Hyden, south-east of Merredin, Western Australia.*

Right middle: *Long and low is the Spalding Hotel, halfway between Jamestown and Clare, South Australia. The terminus of the railway line, Spalding supplies goods and services to nearby graziers and winegrowers.*

Right: *Tarraleah Chalet, 130 kilometres north-west of Hobart on the Nive River, was designed and built by the Hydro-Electric Commission as a showplace for visiting staff and guests from Hobart. The chalet was completed and furnished in 1937 at a cost of £8271 18s 10d.*

The impressive Royal Hotel at Manilla, 45 kilometres north of Tamworth, New South Wales, was built in 1914.

In the heart of sheep- and cattle-growing country, Manilla is at the junction of the Manilla and Namoi Rivers. The town was surveyed in 1860. Nowadays most of the community's business is done at Tamworth.

With little adornment and no advertising, the Criterion Hotel is an important meeting place in the small town of Alpha, between Rockhampton and Longreach, Queensland.

Index

Numerals in *italics* denote colour photographs.

Australia

Australia is many things to many people, infinite in variety and splendour, beautiful, harsh and uncompromising. It is a patient land, vast, full of contrasts, and totally unpredictable.

This book contains over 170 stunning colour photographs of our country from the collection of Douglass Baglin and Yvonne Austin, two of Australia's most accomplished photographers.

With an informative text providing a complete natural history of Australia, this book is a fascinating look at Australia's diversity and the colourful characters who inhabit this wide brown land. 280 x 210 mm, 112 pages.

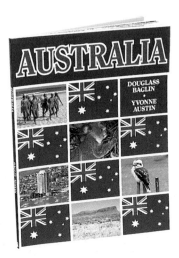

Explore Australia's Great Inland

This is a book about travelling in your own two- or four-wheel-drive vehicle into the outback to places off the beaten track where organised tours seldom venture.

While most places are usually accessible by two-wheel-drive vehicle, others can only be reached by four-wheel drive, especially after rain when roads become muddy quagmires. Additionally, because the more remote outback towns are far apart, fuel stops can be as far between as 200 to 1600 kilometres. Therefore, trips need to be carefully planned and highly organised.

This book tells you all you need to know to explore Australia's Great Inland in safety. It is full of useful information and tips on choice of vehicle, what to take, where to find fuel, how to use communication equipment and on map and compass use. It is beautifully illustrated with over 130 colour pictures and contains all the maps you need.

There are twenty suggested outback trips which provide information on distances, travelling times, road surfaces and vehicle access. Points of interest along the way which are seldom found in tourist brochures are also included.

There are many fascinating places for you to discover in Australia's Great Inland; this book shows you how. 305 x 228 mm, 160 pages.

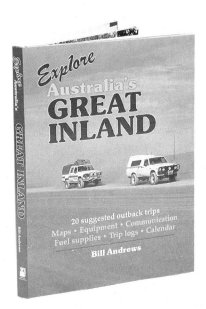

Outback Pubs of Australia

This stunning book contains over fifty of pub artist Rex Newell's favourite paintings. Over the past thirteen years Rex has won national acclaim for his work and is especially well known for his paintings of the old buildings found in the vast Australian Outback.

In the early 1980s Rex held an exhibition of his pub paintings. This was so successful that since this time he has painted nothing but pubs.

For Rex, and indeed for many Australians past and present, the pub is the focal point of Outback life. Fascinated by their atmosphere and architecture, Rex is intrigued by the dilapidated, neglected pubs of the past.

For this book, Rex has searched the Outback, travelling off the beaten track rediscovering the waterholes of the past, and searching out their myths and legends. The carefully researched and anecdotal text complements the paintings making this a lively and interesting book to be enjoyed by all. 305 x 228 mm, 112 pages.

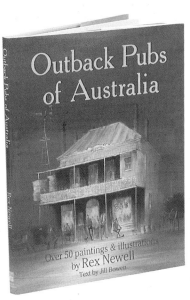

For more information on these and all our publications please see your local bookseller or contact Child & Associates, 5 Skyline Place, Frenchs Forest NSW 2086, phone: (02) 975 1700, fax: (02) 975 1711